POWER AND IMPUNITY
Human rights under the New Order

AI Index: ASA 21/17/94
ISBN: 0 86210 236 7

First published in September 1994 by
Amnesty International Publications
1 Easton Street
London WC1X 8DJ
United Kingdom

Copyright:
   Amnesty International 1994
   Publications
Original language: English

All rights reserved

No part of this publication
may be reproduced, stored
in a retrieval system, or
transmitted in any form or by
any means electronic,
mechanical, photo-
copying, recording and/or
otherwise, without the prior
permission of the publishers.

Printed by: Flashprint Enterprises Ltd.

CONTENTS

INTRODUCTION — 1
Human rights under the New Order:
an overview — 4
International acquiescence — 9

1 A HISTORY OF REPRESSION — 15
The historical setting — 15
    The October 1965 coup — 16
The New Order — 17
    Military power — 18
    Ideological control — 20
    Restrictions on civil and political rights — 21
        Voices of dissent — 23

2 ARMED OPPOSITION AND COUNTER-INSURGENCY — 28
East Timor — 29
Aceh — 31
Irian Jaya — 31
Human rights abuses by opposition groups — 34

3 LAW AND IMPUNITY — 36
A dependent judiciary — 36
Repressive legislation — 37
    The Anti-Subversion Law — 37
    The Hate-sowing Articles — 38
    The Code of Criminal Procedure — 40
Human rights and impunity — 41
    Investigations — 43
    Punishment — 45
    Redress and compensation — 46

4 EXTRAJUDICIAL EXECUTION — 49
East Timor — 50
Aceh — 54
Irian Jaya — 57
Peaceful protesters — 58
    The Nipah dam killings — 58
    The *Haur Koneng* killings — 60
    The killing of Marsinah — 62
Criminal suspects — 64

5 TORTURE, ILL-TREATMENT AND DEATH IN CUSTODY 68
East Timor 69
Aceh 71
Irian Jaya 73
Peaceful protesters 73
Criminal suspects and prisoners 74

6 POLITICAL IMPRISONMENT AND UNFAIR TRIAL 79
Patterns of imprisonment 79
East Timor 83
Aceh 86
Irian Jaya 89
Muslim activists 90
PKI prisoners 92
Students 94
Farmers and land activists 98
Workers and trade unionists 100

7 THE DEATH PENALTY 102
Killing the innocent 103
Cruel treatment 103
Political prisoners 104
Criminal suspects 106

8 GOVERNMENT HUMAN RIGHTS INITIATIVES 110
Shaping the human rights debate 110
Cooperation with UN human rights bodies 112
Restrictions on human rights monitoring 114
The National Human Rights Commission 116
The Government and Amnesty International 117

9 CONCLUSIONS AND RECOMMENDATIONS 120
Recommendations to the Government
  of Indonesia 121
  I. Resolve and redress human rights
    violations 121
  II. Prevent human rights violations 122
  III. Promote human rights 123
Recommendations to UN Member States 124

ENDNOTES 125

GLOSSARY

Aceh Merdeka	—Free Aceh
APEC	—Asia Pacific Economic Cooperation
Apodeti	—Timorese Popular Democratic Association
Bakorstanas	—Coordinating Agency for the Maintenance of National Stability
Brimob	—Police Mobile Brigade
Bupati	—Regent
CGI	—Consultative Group on Indonesia
CNRM	—Maubere Council of National Resistance
DPR	—People's Representative Assembly
Falintil	—East Timorese National Liberation Army
Fretilin	—Revolutionary Front for an Independent East Timor
GPK	—Security Disrupters Movement
ICRC	—International Committee of the Red Cross
IGGI	—Inter-Governmental Group on Indonesia
IPU	—Inter-Parliamentary Union
KODAM	—Regional Military Command
KODIM	—District Military Command
Kopassus	—Special Forces Command
KORAMIL	—Sub-District Military Command
KOREM	—Resort Military Command
KORPRI	—Civil Service Corps of the Republic of Indonesia
KOSTRAD	—Army Strategic Reserve Command
KUHAP	—Code of Criminal Procedure
KUHP	—Criminal Code
LBH	—Legal Aid Institute
Mahmilub	—Special Military Court
MPR	—People's Consultative Assembly
NAM	—Non-Aligned Movement
OPM	—Free Papua Movement
Pancasila	—State ideology of Indonesia
PDI	—Indonesian Democratic Party
Petrus	—"Mysterious killing" campaign
PKI	—Communist Party of Indonesia
POLRI	—Police of the Republic of Indonesia
PPP	—United Development Party
SBSI	—Indonesian Prosperous Workers Union
SPSI	—All Indonesia Workers' Union
UDT	—Timorese Democratic Union

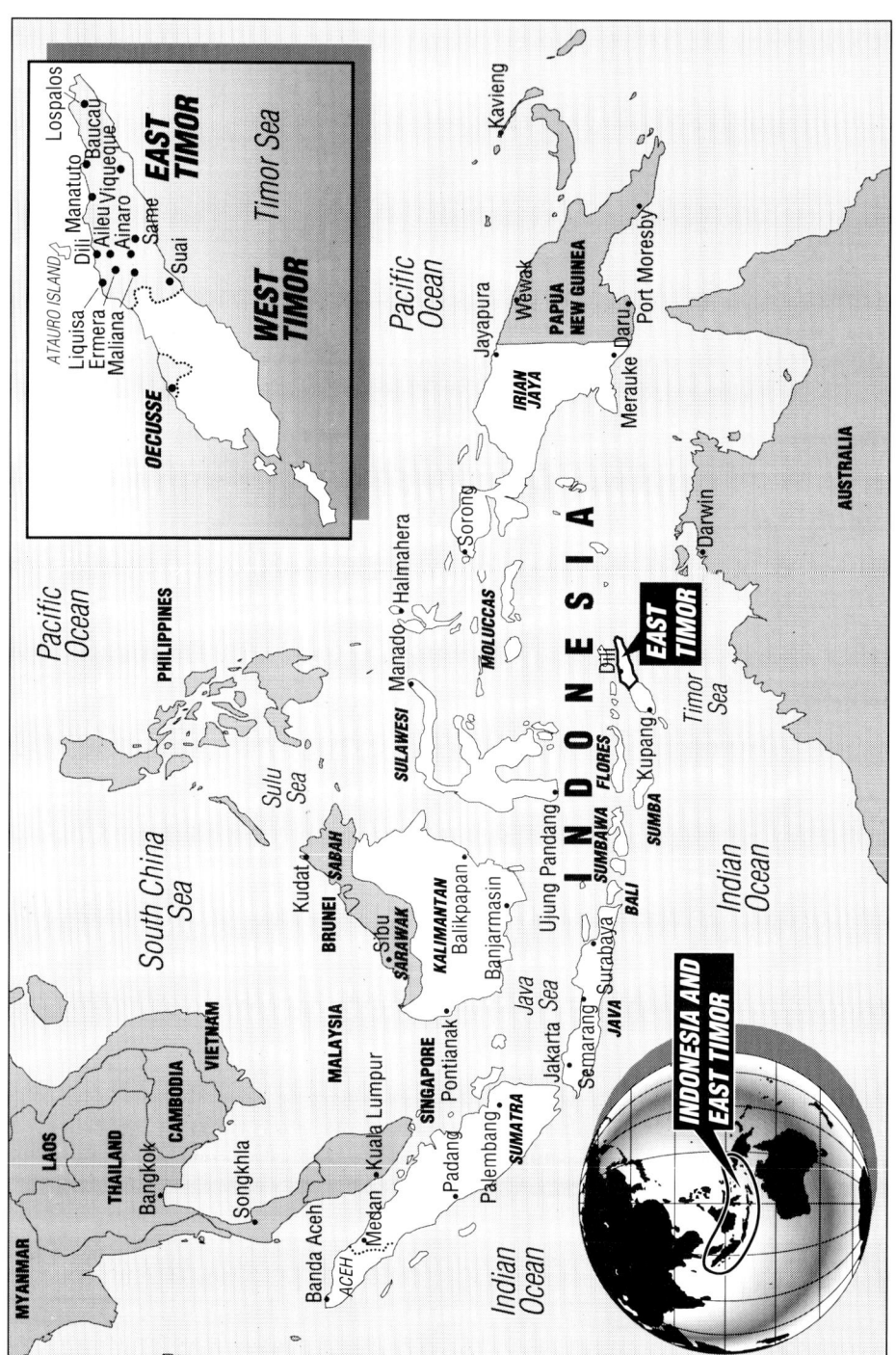

INTRODUCTION

Indonesia's New Order Government has been responsible for human rights violations on a staggering scale since a military coup brought it to power in 1965. Hundreds of thousands of civilians have been killed, their mutilated corpses sometimes left in public places to rot; prisoners, both political and criminal, have been routinely tortured and ill-treated, some so severely that they died or suffered permanent injury; thousands of people have been imprisoned following show trials solely for their peaceful political or religious views; scores of prisoners have been shot by firing-squad, some after more than two decades on death row.

Signs of increasing political openness in Indonesia have recently raised hopes for human rights. However, grave human rights violations continue unabated. In this report Amnesty International examines why the violations continue and why, unless concerted domestic and international pressure is applied on the government, there can be little prospect of real improvement.

This report describes the historical pattern of different kinds of violations — political killing, torture and ill-treatment, political imprisonment and the death penalty — paying particular attention to the period since 1989, when the government began publicly to assert a commitment to protecting human rights. It describes the different groups of people who have been targeted, as well as the official agencies responsible for the violations. Finally, the report contains recommendations which would help to end the most serious violations if the government and the international community were to implement them.

East Timor, the former Portuguese colony invaded by Indonesia in 1975 and still occupied in defiance of United Nations (UN)

POWER AND IMPUNITY

Indonesian soldiers parade their anti-riot equipment past a portrait of President Suharto during celebrations in Jakarta for Armed Forces Day in October 1992. The army has been the dominant political force in Indonesia for the past three decades. © *Reuters*

INTRODUCTION

resolutions, has seen some of the worst violations. The seriousness of the problem was brought home to many in November 1991, when Indonesian troops gunned down as many as 270 peaceful demonstrators at the Santa Cruz cemetery in Dili, the capital. Political killings are not a new phenomenon in East Timor. They are part of a broader pattern of violations which has persisted for nearly 20 years.

Similar patterns of human rights violations have been documented during counter-insurgency operations in Aceh and Irian Jaya where the government faces both peaceful and armed opposition. In these areas, as in East Timor, military authorities have been free to employ virtually any means to maintain national security, order and stability.

Systematic violations have also occurred in parts of Indonesia generally portrayed as stable and harmonious, such as the islands of Java, Sumatra, Bali, Sulawesi and Kalimantan, the regions of Nusa Tenggara and Maluku, and even the capital city, Jakarta. Throughout the country, serious human rights violations have been part of the official response to political opposition and "disorder", and the means of removing perceived obstacles to economic policies. This response has become known in Indonesia as the "security approach".

Wherever they occur, the violations by government forces show a remarkable uniformity. That uniformity stems from certain basic features of the Indonesian political system. The armed forces, and particularly military intelligence and counter-insurgency units, have enormous influence. Counter-insurgency strategies in Indonesia entail both deliberate and unintended violations of human rights. The President and the executive have virtually absolute power which is used arbitrarily, without any effective domestic check. Ideological conformity is enforced at gunpoint. The legal system reflects and reinforces executive and military power, and the judiciary is neither independent nor impartial. Those responsible for human rights violations are almost never brought to justice.

These are the principal factors behind the pattern of human rights violations in Indonesia and East Timor. The violations are not isolated occurrences, nor are they the work of a handful of poorly disciplined soldiers, as the government has sometimes claimed. They are the product of a network of institutions, standard operating procedures and ideological assumptions which underpin

POWER AND IMPUNITY

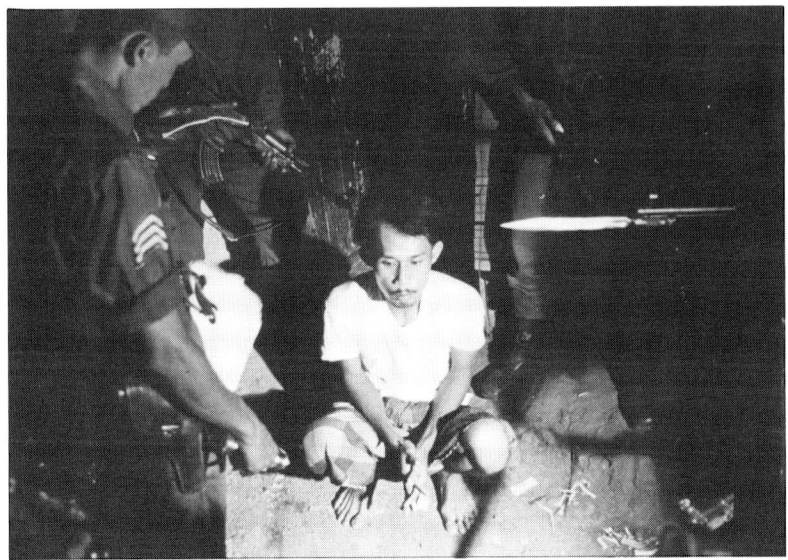

After curfew in a Jakarta street, late 1965. In the wake of the military coup hundreds of thousands of suspected "communists" were hunted down and killed or hauled into custody. © *Rory Dell/Camera Press*

the government's response to expressions of dissent or signs of disorder.

Indonesia became a member of the UN Commission on Human Rights in 1991. The government has since adopted a cynical stance on human rights. In response to criticism at home and abroad it has taken a number of steps to demonstrate its commitment to protecting human rights. It has hosted human rights seminars, established a National Human Rights Commission, and punished a small number of soldiers responsible for human rights violations. At the same time the government has continued to brand human rights activists "subversives" and "enemies of the state". It has also failed to address the root causes of human rights violations. Until this is done, there can be little hope of any real change in the human rights situation.

Human rights under the New Order: an overview

Political killings provide the most dramatic evidence of the magnitude of the human rights problem in Indonesia and East Timor. The slaughter which followed the 1965 coup — between 500,000 and

INTRODUCTION

one million people were killed — appears to have established a precedent for dealing with political opponents. In East Timor 200,000 people, one third of the population, were killed or died of starvation or disease after Indonesia invaded in 1975. In Aceh some 2,000 civilians were killed between 1989 and 1993 during counter-insurgency operations. Hundreds of people have been extrajudicially executed in Irian Jaya over the past 15 years.

The killings have also occurred outside counter-insurgency operations. Soldiers and police have opened fire on peaceful protesters, resulting in hundreds of deaths over the years. Scores of civilians were killed by government troops in the Tanjung Priok area of Jakarta in September 1984, ostensibly in an effort to control a riotous crowd. At least 40 civilians, and possibly as many as 100, were killed in February 1989 when government forces launched a combined land and air assault on a village in Lampung, which the military claimed was harbouring a Muslim rebel gang. In September 1993 soldiers opened fire on a peaceful protest by farmers in Madura, killing four. The list of victims continues to grow.

Convicted criminals have also been singled out and arbitrarily killed. Between 1983 and 1985, government death squads summarily executed an estimated 5,000 alleged criminals in Indonesian cities. In 1989 the President boasted that the killings were deliberate government policy: "shock therapy" to bring crime under control. The government's "mysterious killing" campaign, as it was known, drew to an end in 1986, but police forces have continued to employ excessive force in dealing with suspected criminals. In early 1994, the Jakarta police force launched "Operation Cleansing", aimed at ridding the city of criminal elements before the November summit of the Asia Pacific Economic Cooperation (APEC) forum.

The torture and ill-treatment of political detainees, civilians in areas of rebel activity, and criminal suspects has become commonplace. Many of the victims have died as a result. Torture and ill-treatment have been used to obtain political or military intelligence, to extract confessions, and to terrorize and thereby seek to control individuals or whole communities.

Ever since 1965, arbitrary arrest and detention have formed an essential part of the government's armoury for suppressing dissent, gathering military and political intelligence, and maintaining "order". More than one million people were detained for involvement with the Communist Party of Indonesia (PKI) after the 1965 coup.

POWER AND IMPUNITY

Plainclothes police officers seize an anti-war protester outside the Japanese Embassy in central Jakarta in February 1991. Witnesses said several demonstrators were beaten. Government repression is characterized by tight restrictions on civil and political liberties such as freedom of speech and of assembly. © Reuters

Hundreds of thousands were held without charge or trial for up to 14 years. In recent years, those most likely to be arbitrarily arrested have been alleged rebels or people living in areas of suspected rebel activity. In East Timor the authorities have employed a system of short-term detention, torture and ill-treatment. In other areas victims have been held incommunicado for longer periods without charge or trial. In Aceh several hundreds, possibly thousands, of people were arbitrarily detained by military forces between 1989 and 1993, some of them for up to two years. Only about 50 were ever brought to trial. Peaceful protesters, strikers, farmers, students, and human rights activists have also been arbitrarily detained.

In Indonesia and East Timor more than 3,000 people have been

INTRODUCTION

tried and sentenced to lengthy prison terms, or death, for alleged political crimes since 1965. They include some 1,000 people accused of involvement in the 1965 coup or membership of the PKI, at least 25 of whom are still in jail almost 30 years later. Other political prisoners include some 500 Muslim activists, preachers and scholars; several hundred advocates of independence for East Timor, Aceh and Irian Jaya; and scores of university students, workers, farmers and human rights activists. Many had neither used nor advocated violence. Some 350 political prisoners are still serving sentences of up to life imprisonment.

Political trials in Indonesia and East Timor have consistently fallen short of fair trial standards, and have often not conformed to Indonesia's own Code of Criminal Procedure. This has been particularly true in trials of people charged under the Anti-Subversion Law, which permits the suspension of the minimum guarantees and safeguards contained in the Code of Criminal Procedure. This law carries harsh punishments, including the death penalty. Virtually all political trials in Indonesia and East Timor have been show trials, intended partly to substantiate the claim that the New Order is a state based on the "rule of law", and partly as a warning to potential dissidents. Only one of thousands of defendants is known to have been acquitted of a political crime in Indonesia or East Timor.

The government has also used the judicial death penalty, particularly against its political opponents. Of the 30 people executed since 1985, 27 were political prisoners, most of whom had served more than 20 years in jail. The timing of the executions suggests they were the result of political considerations. The periodic execution of political prisoners has served simultaneously as a reminder of the purported need for "vigilance" against subversion and as an expression of the ultimate power of the state.

Army personnel and members of elite military units, such as the Special Forces Command (*Kopassus*), the paramilitary Police Mobile Brigade (*Brimob*) and the anti-riot squads, have been responsible for most grave violations against suspected political opponents. Fewer abuses are attributed to members of regular police units, mainly because they play a minor role in counter-insurgency operations and in the arrest of political suspects. However, police personnel are chiefly responsible for the torture, ill-treatment and sometimes death, of criminal suspects. Serious violations have also been committed by members of government-

POWER AND IMPUNITY

Woman and child in East Timor, invaded by Indonesia in 1975. The territory is still illegally occupied, in defiance of UN resolutions, and has seen some of the gravest violations of human rights. © Steve Cox

sponsored military and police auxiliary forces, and by prison guards and officials.

The victims of human rights violations in Indonesia and East Timor have come from all religious and ethnic groups, with little regard to age, gender or social standing. But the poor and the dispossessed, including farmers, urban slum dwellers and workers, make up the majority of the victims.

International acquiescence

The international community has, until recently, remained silent in the face of systematic human rights abuse in Indonesia and East Timor. There is a simple reason for this silence: from its inception, Indonesia's New Order government has been an important friend and ally to the West, and has been spared criticism by its Asian neighbours and member states of the Non-Aligned Movement (NAM).

With the fourth largest population in the world, a vast store of natural resources and a huge supply of cheap labour, Indonesia has always been seen as an economic prize. The decimation of the PKI in 1965 and 1966, the overthrow of the militant nationalist Sukarno and his replacement by a staunchly anti-communist military regime dramatically improved economic opportunities and, just as importantly, offered substantial political benefits to the West at the height of the Cold War. Sitting astride critical sea-lanes of Southeast Asia which link the Pacific and Indian Oceans, Indonesia was then, and remains today, of considerable strategic importance. As a result, from 1965 and throughout the Cold War, the United States of America (USA) and many other western countries provided abundant economic, military and political support, and found it expedient to ignore clear evidence of systematic human rights violations.

Since the Cold War ended, the political imperatives of anti-communism have been supplanted by a preoccupation with "democratization" and "good governance". Some western governments have now begun to voice concern about Indonesia's human rights record, particularly in East Timor. Many expressed outrage over the Santa Cruz massacre in November 1991; condemnation followed the sentencing of East Timorese resistance leader Xanana Gusmão in May 1993; and a series of UN resolutions and statements

POWER AND IMPUNITY

Jakarta street scene: this man is transporting scavenged tin and plastic containers to one of the city's many small recycling home industries. Despite rapid industrial growth, many of Indonesia's 185 million people live in poverty. Most victims of human rights violations in Indonesia and East Timor are drawn from the ranks of the poor and the dispossessed. © *AFP*

INTRODUCTION

Muslim women perform their evening prayers at Al Azhar mosque in Jakarta. Eighty-seven per cent of Indonesia's population is Muslim. It is the world's largest Islamic country. Hundreds of Muslims have been jailed over the past 15 years and hundreds more have been killed when security forces have opened fire on peaceful demonstrations. © AFP

in 1992, 1993 and 1994 openly criticized Indonesia for its poor human rights record in East Timor.

In a significant shift from previous practice, some governments have taken concrete measures to underline their human rights concerns. In the aftermath of the Santa Cruz massacre, for example, the Netherlands announced plans to link economic assistance to human rights improvements. Canada and Denmark temporarily froze new development aid commitments, although aid already in the pipeline continued to flow. In 1993 Belgium made bilateral aid commitments conditional on respect for human rights. In mid-1993 Italy ended all military transfers to Indonesia, citing human rights concerns.

The US Congress and Administration have also taken significant steps. In 1992 and again in 1993, Congress cut funds for military education and training to the Indonesian armed forces, subject to substantial improvements in human rights practices. In 1993 Congress prevented the sale of fighter jets to Indonesia on human rights grounds. The US Government has also warned the Indonesian Government that it might lose its trading privileges unless it substantially improves labour rights.

Nevertheless, the international community's response to Indonesia's human rights record leaves much to be desired. Many governments, while publicly professing concern over human rights in Indonesia and East Timor, continue to supply military equipment to Indonesia — equipment which could be used to commit human rights violations. Others have provided military training to, or have conducted joint exercises with, Indonesian armed forces' units well-known for human rights abuse. In 1993 the British Government approved the sale of 40 jet fighters to the Indonesian Government; Germany sold three submarines and 39 other navy vessels, some equipped with missile launchers; and the Swiss Government approved the sale of ammunition and parts for anti-aircraft guns. In mid-1993 the Australian military conducted joint exercises and training with Indonesia's counter-insurgency unit, *Kopassus*, which has been responsible for grave abuses over many years. In October 1993, the European Commission rejected proposals for an embargo on arms sales to Indonesia.

While some governments have linked economic assistance to human rights performance, most aid donors have increased their level of aid to Indonesia. In the two years since the Santa Cruz massacre, the Consultative Group on Indonesia (CGI), a development aid consortium which meets annually to agree bilateral and multilateral development assistance, has consistently increased its total disbursement.[1] Nor has concern for human rights had any noticeable impact on trading patterns. The willingness of foreign governments to conduct business as usual sends a clear signal that human rights take second place to economic interests.

Not only do foreign governments continue to provide economic and military support to the government, they also turn away refugees from repression in Indonesia. Several European governments, including Finland, Sweden and the Vatican, have violated their obligations under international law when dealing with asylum-seekers who sought refuge in their diplomatic premises in Indonesia. Several Asian states, including Japan, Malaysia and Papua New Guinea, have either refused protection to asylum-seekers who entered their embassies, or have forcibly returned them to Indonesia despite the serious risks. Some governments have attempted to justify their actions by citing assurances from the Indonesian

INTRODUCTION

University students watch as a giant effigy of an army boot, symbolizing repression, is set on fire. About 2,000 students attended this protest in Jakarta, in April 1989, against the use of armed force to quell student demonstrations. Hundreds of students have been detained and dozens imprisoned for political reasons. © Reuters

authorities that the asylum-seekers would not be persecuted if returned or transferred. However, official Indonesian assurances of the safety of asylum-seekers have been routinely breached.

An even more fundamental problem is that the international community has focused almost exclusively on the human rights problem in East Timor and, even there, only on the most dramatic incidents such as the Santa Cruz massacre. Grave violations committed by Indonesian forces in Aceh, Irian Jaya, Java, the capital city, Jakarta — and throughout the archipelago — have gone virtually unnoticed. On the few occasions when human rights violations outside East Timor have troubled the international conscience, these have been treated as isolated incidents. This report shows that human rights abuse is not confined to East Timor, and that the killing, torture and political imprisonment reported from various parts of Indonesia are far from isolated incidents; they are part of the pattern of systematic human rights violations which has unfolded over more than a quarter of a century.

1

A history of repression

Systematic human rights abuse is inextricably linked to the structure of political power in Indonesia and specifically to the New Order's military traditions, political institutions and ideological orientation. From the perspective of human rights, the key features of the administration are the considerable political power of the military, the concentration of executive power in the hands of the President and his immediate circle, and the enforcement of a strict ideological conformity.

The absence of any check on presidential and executive power has resulted in the arbitrary use of repressive methods. This pattern has been reinforced by the fact that the security forces have generally been free to use force and to commit human rights violations without fear of punishment.

The historical setting

The territory which constitutes present-day Indonesia was colonized piecemeal by the Netherlands over some 350 years. By the turn of this century, the colony known as the Netherlands East Indies encompassed a vast territory and a range of distinct cultural, religious and linguistic groups. Despite this diversity, by the 1930s an Indonesian nationalist movement had united to challenge Dutch rule. Nationalist forces gained inspiration from the easy defeat of the Dutch colonial regime by Japan in 1942.

Sukarno, the country's first President, proclaimed Indonesia's independence on 17 August 1945, shortly after the Japanese surrender. However, it was not until late 1949, after a four-year fight to resist the return of the Dutch, that the country finally obtained its freedom. The "National Revolution" firmly established the political importance of Indonesia's newly formed armed forces. By the early 1960s, the army was one of three major actors in Indonesian politics; the others were Sukarno and the three-million-strong PKI.

The first 15 years of independence (1950-1965) left important political and human rights legacies. A Constitution promulgated in 1950 guaranteed the full range of civil and political rights enumerated in the Universal Declaration of Human Rights. However, the country's experiment with constitutionalism ended inauspiciously in 1959 when, under pressure from the army, President Sukarno disbanded the Constituent Assembly and restored the 1945 Constitution by decree. The 1945 Constitution, still in force today, offers only vague guarantees of basic human rights and concentrates political power in the hands of the executive, especially the President.

The October 1965 coup

The central political event in Indonesia's post-independence history was the military coup of 1965. On 1 October 1965, a handful of middle-ranking army officers loyal to President Sukarno kidnapped and killed six army generals whom they suspected of collaboration with the US Central Intelligence Agency and disloyalty to the President. Although a handful of PKI leaders may have been aware of the plan, historical evidence shows that the vast majority of PKI members and supporters had no knowledge of it, and played no role in it.

Nevertheless, alleged PKI responsibility for the abortive coup — especially for the murder of the generals — was used by the military, led by General (now President) Suharto, as a pretext to stage a successful counter-coup. This was the prelude to one of the worst massacres of this century. In less than one year, between 500,000 and one million people were killed. The mass killings were not a spontaneous reaction to the supposed treachery of the PKI, as the government and the military has always claimed; they were encouraged, organized and carried out by the Indonesian army and by vigilante groups acting with military support or acquiescence.

Indonesia's current government rode to power in the wake of the October coup; nearly 30 years later, the coup still influences Indonesia's political life, and official human rights policy and practice. The official myth of PKI responsibility continues to sustain virulent anti-communism, and to justify the repression of political opposition. The idea that the PKI "betrayed" the nation has meant that those who killed alleged communists are revered as national heroes, at least by those currently in power. According to official history, the guilty are not those who ordered the killing of hundreds of thousands of civilians, but the victims themselves.

The New Order

General Suharto emerged the dominant political figure after the 1965 coup. Backed by the army and a variety of anti-communist political groups, he effectively took control of the country, and was declared President in March 1968. Since then, he has stood unopposed in five successive elections, most recently in 1993.

Presidential power is reflected in the broad powers granted to other parts of the executive. Members of the President's inner circle, whether cabinet members or military officers, enjoy virtually unchecked power. Executive control is exercised through a massive and highly centralized state bureaucracy, which extends down to village level. Despite government rhetoric about popular participation in development, the country is run by executive decision channelled through the state bureaucracy.

Presidential and executive power has been further consolidated through undermining other political institutions. Outside of the dominant government-backed party, Golkar, only two political parties are allowed to exist, neither of which has any chance of winning a majority.[2] Before national elections, held every five years, all candidates must be screened by military intelligence agencies, and approved by the President. Candidates deemed ideologically unsound are barred. Political party activity is illegal between elections. Golkar is officially linked to the military, the executive, and the civil service. All state employees and officials are required to support it.

The main parliamentary body, the People's Consultative Assembly (MPR), meets every five years to elect the President and to approve an outline of state policy. Only 400 of its 1,000 members are elected. The others are appointed by the President and the military. The armed forces' appointees and the elected representatives also sit in the People's Representative Assembly (DPR). The DPR is formally the country's legislative body, but its chief function is to rubber-stamp laws tabled by the executive. Provincial and sub-provincial parliamentary bodies are similarly powerless.

POWER AND IMPUNITY

Troops on the streets of Jakarta during the 1982 election. The New Order Government claims to be a democracy based on the rule of law, but in most respects it is a military authoritarian government. © *Paul Forster/Impact*

Military power

After the 1965 coup the army became the dominant political force. The institutions and the ideology of the Indonesian state have since been moulded by the military, and its leadership composed of military officers. The New Order Government claims to be a democracy based on the rule of law; in most respects it is a military authoritarian government. This has had important consequences for human rights policy and practice.

The methods employed by the military and paramilitary bodies to destroy the PKI were institutionalized after the 1965 coup. Similar methods have been used in successive counter-insurgency campaigns and in numerous operations to restore "order". The use of force and intensive surveillance in response to perceived threats to national security, has been officially termed "the security approach". Opposition groups, and even some elements within the government, have begun to question this approach in recent years. However, there is little indication that the military is prepared to relinquish its grip on the country's political life, or to abandon the repressive methods which keep it in power.

CHAPTER 1

Indonesian soldiers training in East Timor. Troops are deployed down to village level throughout Indonesia and East Timor. The Indonesian army is organized to deal primarily with domestic opposition to the government rather than external threats. © Steve Cox

The Indonesian military has always been organized to deal with domestic rather than international threats. Troops are deployed throughout the country, under a territorial structure which penetrates down to village level. At each level, the military has wide-ranging authority over political, social, and economic, as well as conventionally military, matters. In principle, the armed forces work with the civilian bureaucracy, but in practice the word of the military commander is law.

The army's territorial forces are complemented by a range of elite combat and paramilitary units, which are principally deployed in counter-insurgency operations. All are responsible for grave human rights violations. The most powerful are the *Kopassus* units which have been responsible for some of the worst violations in Indonesia's history. Other counter-insurgency forces include the paramilitary *Brimob*, the Army Strategic Reserve Command (*KOSTRAD*), and the Police Riot Squad.

At the core of the military apparatus is a pervasive intelligence network, operating through normal command structures, and through a number of semi-autonomous agencies. One of the most powerful of these is the Coordinating Agency for the Maintenance of National Stability (*Bakorstansas*). The dominance of the intelligence apparatus within the armed forces has encouraged the development of a highly intensive system of state surveillance of ordinary citizens, which has facilitated human rights violations.

Ideological control

The government has not depended exclusively on overt violence to achieve its aims. It has also relied on tight ideological control. At the core of this system are the state ideology, *Pancasila*, the 1945 Constitution, and key "national goals" such as national stability, security and order. These goals are portrayed as so fundamental that any threat to them justifies the use of "firm measures", including violence, by the state. Despite official rhetoric about democracy and political openness, it is the executive and the military authorities who define and interpret the "national goals" and determine when they have been threatened. As the Chief of the State Intelligence Coordinating Agency explained in February 1994: "Local human rights groups are alright so long as they do not deviate from the official policy line".[3]

Pancasila embodies five principles: belief in one God, humanitarianism, national unity, democracy and social justice. Criticism of or deviation from *Pancasila* is punishable by law. According to Law No. 8 of 1985 all social organizations must adopt *Pancasila* as their sole ideology. When it was tabled the law provoked a storm of protest, principally from the religious and human rights community. Some of the protesters were arrested and sentenced to lengthy prison terms for subversion.

The preoccupation with national security, stability and order, and the enforcement of strict ideological conformity, contribute to human rights violations, by restricting fundamental civil and political rights, and by providing a veneer of legality behind which to hide blatant abuses. Advocates of independence for East Timor, Aceh and Irian Jaya; farmers who resist the expropriation of their land; writers who challenge the state's interpretation of history; Muslim preachers who criticize *Pancasila*; workers who exercise their right to strike; activists who call for democratization; students and human rights lawyers who criticize government development policy; and urban squatters and traders who create "disorder" by their mere existence, are all vulnerable to accusations of being "subversives", "communists", "terrorists" or "traitors". This puts

CHAPTER 1

them at risk of arbitrary detention, torture, imprisonment or death, a powerful deterrent to all but the most courageous.

The importance which the New Order attaches to ideological control can be judged by the violence of its reaction to any challenge, however peaceful. Human rights violations often occur in response to essentially peaceful protests. The Santa Cruz massacre in East Timor was officially justified on the grounds that demonstrators were expressing anti-government sentiments. In July 1992 the Regional Military Commander, Major General Mantiri, told the press:

> "We don't regret anything. What happened was quite proper...They were opposing us, demonstrating, even yelling things against the government. To me that is identical with rebellion, so that is why we took firm action...I don't think there's anything strange in that."[4]

Talk of increased openness has given a slightly different gloss to political debate in Indonesia since the early 1990s, but it has not significantly altered the underlying pattern of ideological control. Senior officials express enthusiasm for democratization and human rights protection, but at the same time warn of their inherent threat to national security and stability. The advocates of "western-style human rights", liberal democracy, and environmental protection, are described as subversives and even labelled "fourth generation communists".

In December 1993, only months after calling for greater political openness, the President accused peaceful pro-democracy protesters of being communists in disguise and called for public vigilance:

> "They are asking for more freedom to serve their own interests and are willing to sacrifice the larger interests. That is against Pancasila...This is a warning for us to beware of the PKI...The name is different but it is the same movement. We have to stay alert.... ".[5]

Restrictions on civil and political rights

Government repression is also characterized by heavy restrictions on a wide range of internationally recognized civil and political rights, such as the freedoms of speech, assembly, conscience, and movement. These restrictions have helped to create an atmosphere

21

of fear; dissent is seldom openly expressed. They have also provided the context for further human rights violations.

Dozens of books are banned each year on the grounds that they express views critical of the government or *Pancasila*, that they contain elements of "Marxist" teachings, or that they might cause public disorder. Those found in possession of banned books are arrested, and some have been sentenced to long prison terms. Among the fictional works currently banned are those of one of Indonesia's foremost authors, Pramoedya Ananta Toer, a former political prisoner. Non-fictional works on politics, religion, law and human rights have also been banned. In 1992 a report on the political trials in Aceh, prepared by the independent Legal Aid Institute (LBH), was banned on the grounds that it portrayed the military authorities in a negative light and could provoke instability. In 1994 the authorities banned a book which argued that President Suharto had masterminded the 1965 coup.

The government also imposes temporary bans on public performances and meetings, including theatrical productions, poetry readings, films, lectures, seminars and peaceful political gatherings. Seeking to explain a gagging order imposed on the poet Emha Ainun Najib in 1991, Central Java's military commander stated:

> *"We have rules. As long as opinions expressed are concerned with differences over implementation, there is no problem. But if they venture into matters concerning* Pancasila, *that is no longer a question of differences of opinion, and there are sanctions ... We hope for openness, but openness of course has limits. If it goes beyond the system that we have arranged, then it is not allowed."*[6]

The domestic and international media also operate under restrictions, although the government has developed a system which requires minimal intervention. Censorship usually takes the form of a warning telephone call or visit from Ministry of Information officials or military intelligence. This is supplemented by selective legal action against those who overstep the mark. By revoking the licences of a few publications or denying visas to foreign journalists, and by detaining or imprisoning a handful of journalists and editors, the authorities have encouraged "self-censorship". Restrictions on the press are heaviest where government forces are conducting counter-insurgency operations, but even in areas of relative stability journalists encounter official obstruction.

CHAPTER 1

The New Order professes a strong commitment to religious freedom, but severely limits this in law and in practice. The state recognizes only five religious faiths — Islam, Catholicism, Protestantism, Buddhism and Hinduism — and acts as the final arbiter and enforcer of religious orthodoxy. The government has banned or disbanded hundreds of religious groups and sects over the years — 517 between 1949 and 1992, according to the Attorney General[7] — and it has arrested members of such groups on charges of subversion and of involvement in illegal organizations. Under the auspices of protecting national security and public order, government and military authorities have also interfered directly, sometimes with force, in the internal affairs of authorized religious bodies.

The government has for many years maintained a "blacklist" of people who may not leave the country. Many were "blacklisted" because of their non-violent political activities or beliefs, and their criticism of the government. A government minister explained in 1991: "...the travel ban is imposed on people who, both here and abroad, threatened the 1945 Constitution and the *Pancasila* state ideology, national development and the government's authority."[8] In addition, hundreds of Indonesian and foreign nationals are not permitted to enter the country because of their real or alleged political beliefs.

Responding to demands for the abolition of "blacklisting", the government passed a new Immigration Law in early 1992. This effectively formalized existing procedures, while adding a number of minor safeguards. In early 1994 the government announced that 15,000 people had been removed from the "blacklist", including 11 prominent opposition figures, many of whom had been "blacklisted" for more than a decade.[9] These were welcome initiatives, but concern remained that the practice of "blacklisting" itself had not been abolished. More importantly, the new law and the reduction in the numbers on the official blacklist — to some 2,000 — did not affect tens of thousands of former PKI prisoners who, under different regulations, have been barred from leaving the country since their release.

Voices of dissent

Official repression has not crushed dissent and opposition. Peaceful opposition to the government and its policies has come from a range of social and political groups, including Muslim activists,

POWER AND IMPUNITY

Farmers protest outside the national parliament building in Jakarta in March 1991. The farmers, from a West Java village, were seeking fair compensation for their land, earmarked for the construction of a golf course. Hundreds of farmers have been forced from their land to make way for real estate and development projects, and some have suffered human rights violations for protesting. © AFP

Workers on strike at PT Sumito, Sidoardjo, East Java, in 1993. Despite heavy restrictions on the right to strike and to organize, Indonesia has seen a rising tide of industrial unrest in the past three years, and scores of trade unionists have been arrested.

CHAPTER 1

retired statesmen and army officers, intellectuals, students, farmers, and trade unionists.

Restrictions on civil and political rights have made it difficult, or unproductive, for these groups to express their views through the normal political channels. As a result, they have often voiced their opinions informally, in demonstrations and wildcat strikes, through literature, theatrical performance or in the formation of autonomous religious communities. Their failure to conform has provided a pretext for heavy-handed police or military intervention in the name of stability and order.

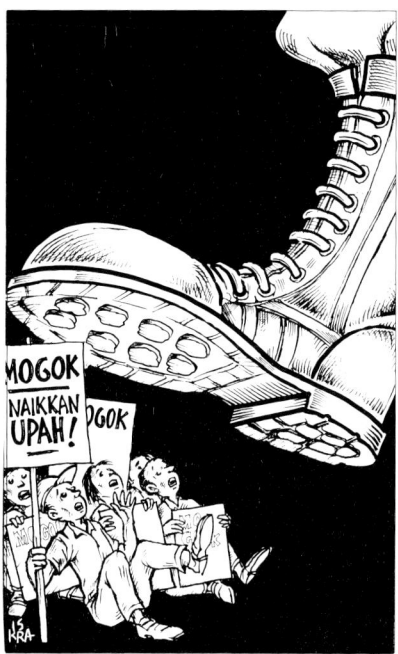

The placard reads "On strike — raise wages!" © Yayak

Eighty-seven per cent of Indonesia's population is Muslim, making it the largest Islamic country in the world. Despite its status as a majority religion, Islam in Indonesia has often been a focus of dissent against the government. In the first decades after independence, various Islamic groups challenged the secularism of the new state, sometimes by resorting to violence. These struggles left a legacy of concern about the possibility of an Islamic threat to the state.

In recent times, the political challenge from Islam has

more often been expressed peacefully. In the mid-1980s Muslim scholars and activists openly criticized official economic and social policy and questioned the enforcement of ideological uniformity at the expense of Islamic teachings. The government reacted by detaining hundreds of Muslim leaders and enacting legislation aimed at defusing the political power of Islam. In the past five years, however, the approach has changed. The President and his circle have tried to woo influential Islamic leaders and intellectuals. Nevertheless, Islam continues to provide a basis for opposition to certain government policies.

Significant opposition has also come from a group of moderate dissidents drawn from the ranks of retired military officers and politicians, intellectuals and influential religious figures. Among the most prominent dissident groups in the past decade has been the "Petition of Fifty", named after a petition which it submitted to the legislature in 1980 in protest at the government's unconstitutional and authoritarian style of leadership. Members of the group were subsequently "blacklisted". In 1993 a former admiral, responsible for "blacklisting" them, stated: "[Their statements] would have undermined our efforts in obtaining aid. So we barred them as a preventive step."[10]

Students and young people have also played a key role in Indonesian politics. After the 1965 coup, they were an essential part of the military-civilian coalition that brought about the destruction of the PKI and the demise of President Sukarno. During the 1970s they began increasingly to play a role as a voice of opposition against the New Order, culminating in a series of anti-government demonstrations in 1974 and again in 1978 and 1979. Wary of their power, the government jailed student leaders and passed legislation to limit their involvement in politics.

This effectively quelled student political activism during the 1980s. However, in the atmosphere of increased political openness of the early 1990s, students and young people once again began to play an important role in politics, organizing demonstrations and campaigns with workers, farmers and others. Students have also supported broader campaigns for human rights and democratization. These activities have led them increasingly into conflict with the New Order; dozens have been jailed as a result.

In recent years, scores of communities have been forced from their land to make way for real estate and development projects. Many of these communities have organized against eviction or to

CHAPTER 1

demand fair compensation for the land they occupy. Most of these protests have been non-violent, but the authorities have used a variety of repressive measures — including intimidation, short-term detention, imprisonment and ill-treatment — to stop them, and have accused "third parties" of using land issues for subversive political ends.

Labour activists have also been accused of having subversive political motives, particularly in the past three years as Indonesia has experienced a rising tide of labour unrest. The government imposes heavy restrictions on the right to strike and to form and join trade unions. Only one trade union federation is recognized, the government-sponsored All Indonesia Workers' Union (SPSI). The government has used various methods, including intimidation and arrest, to undermine independent unions such as the Indonesian Prosperous Workers' Union (SBSI). Direct military and police intervention is routine, even in the most peaceful labour disputes. Military authorities sometimes resort to ill-treatment, torture, including rape, and killing in order to silence workers and labour activists. However, military intervention is usually less violent. Vocal workers are summoned to military headquarters, accused of communist sympathies, and threatened with imprisonment or physical violence unless they "resign" from their jobs.

In recent years, strikers have called mainly for improvements in working conditions and wages which, at the equivalent of about US$1.50 per day, are among the lowest in Asia. Some have also demanded freedom to organize, an end to military intervention in labour disputes and proper investigations into past human rights abuses against workers. These concerns have been echoed by the office of the US Trade Representative which, in June 1993, warned that tariff benefits granted to Indonesian exports might be suspended unless there were significant improvements in the protection of internationally recognized labour rights.

2

Armed opposition and counter-insurgency

The Indonesian Government has faced long-term opposition from groups seeking independence for East Timor, Aceh and Irian Jaya. It has responded with intensive counter-insurgency operations. In these situations, serious human rights violations — already routine under conditions of relative calm and political stability — have been more or less inevitable. Armed opposition groups have also been responsible for serious human rights abuses.

Counter-insurgency campaigns in Aceh, East Timor and Irian Jaya display a chilling uniformity. Normal legal procedures are relaxed or simply ignored by the authorities, and the protection of human rights — limited at the best of times — is subordinated to the exigencies of national security, stability and national unity. Members of the security forces, and others acting with their support, feel free to commit human rights violations with impunity. These problems are compounded by certain characteristics of the Indonesian armed forces, and in particular of its elite counter-insurgency units.

The territorial structure of the armed forces facilitates intensive surveillance, check-points, dawn-to-dusk curfews, house raids, and large-scale arrests. When elite troops are deployed, the incidence of grave violations increases dramatically. This is partly because the methods, traditions and mandate of these units entail the use of all possible means to crush resistance. It is also because their arrival signifies a shift in the balance of political power in the area. Elite troops are deployed on direct orders from the President and the Armed Forces Commander. Under such circumstances, the political authority of the military becomes almost unchallengeable; virtually any means may be used to destroy the "enemy".

CHAPTER 2

A central element of Indonesian counter-insurgency strategy is "civil-military cooperation", officially known as the "People's total defence and security system". Under normal conditions, this is a means of monitoring the community and identifying political opponents. The dangers to civilians forced to cooperate with the military are especially evident in situations of civil conflict. In East Timor and Aceh it has resulted in a tactic known as the "fence of legs", in which villagers are forced to sweep an area ahead of troops, to flush out rebels and to inhibit them from returning fire.

Local vigilante groups and night patrols made up of civilians but run by the military are the lynch-pin of these operations. They are usually composed of between 20 and 30 young men from villages in suspected rebel areas. In the words of a local military commander in Aceh: "The youths are the front line. They know best who the [rebels] are. We then settle the matter."[11]

The strategy also takes the form of military campaigns encouraging civilians to spy on, report, or kill suspected rebels. In November 1990 the newly appointed Regional Military Commander in Aceh, Major General H.R. Pramono, said:

"I have told the community, if you find a terrorist, kill him. There's no need to investigate him. Don't let people be the victims. If they don't do as you order them, shoot them on the spot, or butcher them. I tell members of the community to carry sharp weapons, a machete or whatever. If you meet a terrorist, kill him."[12]

East Timor

The island of Timor lies some 400 miles to the north of Australia and about 1,300 miles from Jakarta. The eastern part of the island, East Timor, was a Portuguese colony until 1975. In November 1975, following a brief civil war, the Revolutionary Front for an Independent East Timor (*Fretilin*) declared East Timor's independence. The following month, on the pretext of ending the civil war, Indonesian forces invaded the territory and have occupied it ever since.

Indonesia declared East Timor its 27th province in July 1976, but its sovereignty has never been recognized by the UN. Some governments, such as the USA, have given *de facto* recognition to Indonesia's claim; the Australian Government has formally recognized Indonesian sovereignty. However, by mid-1994, the people

Indonesian soldier on patrol in East Timor © Steve Cox

of East Timor had yet to exercise a free and fair act of self-determination.

Armed and peaceful opposition to Indonesian rule has continued since 1975 in spite of a massive Indonesian military presence and widespread human rights violations. For much of that time, resistance was spearheaded by *Fretilin*, and its armed wing *Falintil*. In the late 1980s a united front — the Maubere Council of National Resistance (CNRM) — was formed, which incorporated *Fretilin*, the Timorese Democratic Union (UDT) and other pro-independence groups. Although a small guerrilla force still operates in East Timor, most opposition to Indonesian rule takes the form of non-violent underground resistance by farmers, students, young people and civil servants.

The Indonesian Government has repeatedly announced plans to withdraw troops from the territory. However, according to official military figures, nine army battalions — some 6,000 troops — were deployed in the territory in early 1994. One battalion was withdrawn in late 1993, but was replaced almost immediately by other forces, including 200 combat troops of the elite Strategic Reserve Command (KOSTRAD), and a unit of the Police Mobile Brigade (*Brimob*).

Aceh

Aceh, with a population of 3.4 million, lies at the northern tip of the island of Sumatra, about 1,000 miles from Jakarta. The site of one of the earliest Islamic sultanates in southeast Asia, Aceh has a rich cultural heritage and a long tradition of resistance to domination by outside authorities. That tradition was rekindled by the armed independence group, *Aceh Merdeka* (Free Aceh), which unilaterally declared Aceh's independence on 4 December 1976.[13] Popular support for independence has been fuelled in recent years by resentment over the unequal benefits of industrial development in the area, and a perceived lack of respect for local custom and religion by central government and military authorities, and economic migrants.

By 1989 *Aceh Merdeka* had gained the sympathy of a significant cross-section of the population, particularly in the northeast. However, counter-insurgency operations begun in mid-1990 dramatically reduced the group's room for manoeuvre in the countryside, thereby weakening its military position. In March 1991 government and military authorities claimed that *Aceh Merdeka* had been "crushed" and by the end of the year many of the group's key field commanders had been killed or captured. Nevertheless, *Aceh Merdeka* continued to mount sporadic attacks on military and police targets.

Irian Jaya

When Indonesia became independent in 1949, Irian Jaya — then known as Netherlands New Guinea — remained under Dutch control. *De facto* authority was transferred to Indonesia on 1 May 1963 and in 1969 the government held a plebiscite to determine the territory's political status. Despite substantial opposition the plebiscite produced a vote for integration.

Opposition to integration with Indonesia has continued since 1963. Real and perceived cultural and racial differences between the indigenous Melanesians of Irian Jaya and settlers from other parts of Indonesia have been an important source of the political

POWER AND IMPUNITY

Indonesian troops on patrol in Banda Aceh. Some 2,000 civilians were killed by government forces during counter-insurgency operations against the armed opposition group Aceh Merdeka between 1989 and 1993. © Tempo

Civilians being trained by the army to combat "security disruptors" in Aceh. The dangers to civilians forced to cooperate with the military are especially evident in situations of civil conflict. In East Timor and Aceh it has resulted in a tactic known as the "fence of legs", in which villagers are forced to sweep an area ahead of troops, to flush out rebels and to inhibit them from returning fire. © Tempo

CHAPTER 2

*Road development project in Irian Jaya. Economic development and destruction of natural resources has led to widespread protest. Among the most prominent groups advocating independence has been the Free Papua Movement (*OPM*). The* OPM *advocates armed opposition to the Indonesian Government, but many supporters of independence have employed peaceful means.* © *Michael K. Nichols/Magnum*

tension. The resettlement of Indonesian migrants in Irian Jaya, known as "transmigration", has been criticized as an official drive to colonize and assimilate the local population. The exploitation of the territory's natural resources by government-owned and private commercial interests has also caused concern over traditional rights and environmental degradation. This has fuelled opposition to Indonesian rule.

Among the most prominent groups advocating independence has been the Free Papua Movement (OPM). The number of OPM fighters is officially estimated at a few hundred, but the number of people who sympathize with the group is much greater. The OPM advocates armed struggle, but many supporters of independence have employed peaceful means, including demonstrations, flag-raising ceremonies, political discussion groups, and appeals to the UN and other international bodies.

Human rights abuses by opposition groups

All three main armed opposition groups in Indonesia and East Timor are reported to have committed human rights abuses, including deliberate and arbitrary killing, torture and hostage taking. Access to the areas concerned is strictly limited and information about opposition abuses is seldom well-documented, so such reports are difficult to verify. Nevertheless, Amnesty International believes they must be treated with the utmost seriousness.

Indonesian authorities have frequently accused *Fretilin* supporters of human rights abuses, such as the torture and execution of suspected informers. They have usually failed to provide sufficient detail about the alleged abuse to allow proper assessment of its veracity. However, through independent channels, Amnesty International has received several well-documented reports of opposition abuse. One case, announced by *Fretilin* itself, was the deliberate execution, in 1983, of a number of East Timorese alleged to have collaborated with Indonesian forces. Opposition abuses appear to have continued in more recent years, but on a much reduced scale.

Indonesian military statements and local press reports attributed serious human rights abuses to *Aceh Merdeka* in 1989 and 1990. Initially, the victims were police and military personnel. Until April 1990 only one civilian, a suspected informer, was reported to have been killed by *Aceh Merdeka*. The pattern shifted in mid-1990 with increasing attacks on civilians. Official reports of attacks on civilians increased dramatically in May 1990 and escalated in June, just before the government announced the deployment of additional counter-insurgency troops in the area. The principal victims were suspected collaborators and non-Acehnese living in transmigration sites in Aceh Timur and Aceh Utara. By the end of June, at least 30 civilians had been killed and thousands of transmigrants had fled their homes following threats and intimidation allegedly from *Aceh Merdeka* members.

In Irian Jaya, OPM members are said to have been responsible for an armed attack on a transmigration site near Jayapura in March 1988, in which at least 13 civilians were killed and some 17 others wounded. Another OPM attack on two transmigration sites in December 1989 resulted in the deaths of at least three people. In November 1990, OPM guerillas captured six people, including two foreign missionaries, at Amanab in Papua New Guinea, and held them hostage for nearly two weeks, demanding Papua New Guinea's recognition of the independent state of "West Papua".

Amnesty International condemns such abuses, and calls upon the leadership of the three main armed opposition groups to halt such practices and to abide by the principles of international humanitarian law. However, the actions of armed opposition groups, no matter how violent, can never be used to justify human rights violations by government forces. Governments bear a unique responsibility to uphold and protect human rights. If they show contempt for human rights, others are likely to feel free to do likewise.

3

Law and impunity

Indonesian government and military authorities claim the New Order is based on the rule of law rather than political power. This is only partly true. Like any legal system, Indonesia's both reflects and sustains the prevailing structure of political power. The dominance of the military and the executive in Indonesia are manifest in four related aspects of the legal system: the lack of an independent judiciary; repressive laws and regulations; the arbitrary implementation of the law; and the failure to bring human rights violators to justice.

A dependent judiciary

In law, the Indonesian judiciary is independent of the executive; the reality is very different. Limitations on judicial independence are particularly evident in political cases, where the military has unquestioned authority, public prosecutors do the government's bidding, and judges avoid rulings which would embarrass the government or the security forces.

This lack of independence is partly an institutional problem. The courts are administered by the Ministry of Justice. Judges, court officials and public prosecutors are therefore dependent on the executive branch for their salaries, promotions and other benefits. Those who defy the executive and the military may find their career prospects limited.

Several laws and regulations undermine the independence of the judiciary. All government employees, including judges, must be members of the sole civil servant's organization, KORPRI, which operates under the auspices of the powerful Ministry of Home Affairs. The President may intervene directly in judicial matters, by indicating cases which he wishes to see pursued. The Supreme Court may determine whether government decrees and instructions conform with basic laws, but does not have the power of full judicial review.

The judiciary's lack of independence is more than an institutional or legal problem. Even where the system provides formal guarantees of autonomy and impartiality, these are routinely undermined, particularly by the military. Whatever the law may say, the judiciary is an arm of the regime. This has been evident in virtually all political trials, in pre-trial hearings, and in the fact that the perpetrators of human rights violations are seldom brought to justice.

Repressive legislation

A wide array of repressive laws and regulations have been used to imprison, and even put to death, real or alleged political opponents, and to warn potential dissidents against opposition. The laws also contain procedural provisions which encourage other violations. Significant improvements in new laws on the judiciary and in the new Code of Criminal Procedure have been undermined by official indifference and non-compliance.

The current Criminal Code is inherited from the colonial period. Conscious of the need to rid the legal system of the legacy of the past, the government has undertaken to amend it. This initiative is unlikely to have an impact on the bulk of Indonesia's repressive legislation. The Draft Criminal Code, currently under review, incorporates virtually all previous national security laws without significant amendment. In any case, much of the most repressive legislation is contained in presidential and ministerial decrees, directives and decisions, which are largely unaffected by the Criminal Code.

The Anti-Subversion Law

A cornerstone of Indonesia's repressive legislation is the Anti-Subversion Law. Originally promulgated as a Presidential Decree in 1963, this law has been used to justify the detention without trial of hundreds of thousands of alleged government opponents, and to put thousands more through show trials. The vague and sweeping language of the law permits the prosecution and conviction of anyone whose words or actions can be construed as disruptive of public order, or critical of *Pancasila*, the government, its institutions or its polices.

The Anti-Subversion Law also facilitates other human rights violations, such as incommunicado detention, torture, "disappearance" and extrajudicial execution. Key provisions of the Code of Criminal Procedure designed to protect the rights of detainees either do not apply, or are commonly ignored, when the authorities invoke the Anti-Subversion Law. It provides harsher penalties than other laws on political crimes, including the death penalty. The standards of evidence required to produce a conviction for subversion are also much less rigorous, so that the law is commonly used where the authorities cannot find adequate evidence. The exceptional powers granted to the military and the prosecution under this law, and the heavy restrictions it imposes on detainees' rights, make serious human rights violations almost inevitable.

Lawyers, parliamentarians, and international human rights experts, including the UN Special Rapporteur on torture, have called repeatedly for the repeal of the Anti-Subversion Law. Some claim that it is unconstitutional, others that its content contravenes prevailing legal principles and norms. All agree that it has been an instrument of repression.

The Anti-Subversion Law continues to be widely used; both government and judicial authorities have opposed its abolition. Government officials have actually argued for extending the law's scope. Their arguments reveal the dangers inherent in this law. Responding to calls for abolition in early 1993, the Attorney General accused the abolitionists of subversion:

"*Those who say that the Anti-Subversion Law is unpopular, are those who have the intention of committing subversive acts themselves.*"[14]

There are indications that the Anti-Subversion Law will be incorporated, with minor revisions, into the new Criminal Code. In practice this is unlikely to make much difference; it may simply give the law more permanence and legitimacy. The only way to impose limits is to get rid of the law altogether, for it has proved utterly subject to abuse.

The Hate-sowing Articles

A series of articles which forbid "spreading hatred" against government officials are also due to be retained in the new Criminal Code.

CHAPTER 3

Demonstration in August 1993 against the trial of two students accused of showing hostility to the government. The Hate-sowing Articles (Haatzaai Artikelen) have been used to imprison dozens of prisoners of conscience.
© AFP

The Hate-sowing Articles (*Haatzaai Artikelen*) were introduced by the Dutch colonial administration in the early 1900s and, with the rest of the colonial criminal code, were incorporated into Indonesia's Criminal Code after independence. Faced with strong criticism of the Anti-Subversion Law, the government has recently turned to the Hate-sowing Articles to imprison, or to intimidate, alleged political opponents.

Articles 154, 155 and 160 are frequently used to suppress dissent. Under Article 154, "...the public expression of feelings of hostility, hatred or contempt toward the government..." is punishable by up to seven years' imprisonment. Article 155 prohibits the expression of such feelings or views through the public media, with a maximum penalty of four-and-a-half years' imprisonment. Article 160 prescribes a maximum of six years' imprisonment for "inciting" others to disobey a government order or to break the law. Article 134, although not usually described as one of the Hate-sowing Articles, punishes "insulting the President" with a maximum sentence of six years' imprisonment. Dozens of peaceful protestors have been jailed as prisoners of conscience under these articles.

The Code of Criminal Procedure

It is not only repressive laws which have contributed to the human rights problem in Indonesia, but the often arbitrary way in which even the best laws have been implemented. Laws which provide some protection for detainees or defendants are often emasculated by official regulations on their implementation. Even in the absence of such regulations, laws which protect the rights of ordinary citizens or which circumscribe the power of the state, are frequently ignored by government and military officials. This is most evident in the implementation of the Code of Criminal Procedure.

Introduced in 1981, the Code of Criminal Procedure was justly hailed by legal experts as a significant improvement over its predecessor, particularly in the protection it offered the rights of detainees and defendants. In practice, key provisions in the Code are often ignored, or their implementation obstructed. For example, detainees are entitled to have a lawyer but many do not have one at the time of interrogation. Police and military authorities regularly deny detainees access to relatives and lawyers and obstruct their efforts to provide legal aid.

The effectiveness of the provisions in the Code are undermined by Ministry of Justice guidelines for their implementation. One guideline stipulates that suspects may have access to a lawyer only during working hours; interrogation frequently occurs at night, outside working hours. Moreover, the Code does not require investigating authorities to inform legal counsel of their intention to interrogate a suspect, and as a matter of course they prefer not to do so. Another ministerial guideline requires that a prison official be present during conversations between detainees and their lawyers, whereas the Code indicates that lawyers should be free to talk in confidence with their clients in prison.

The guarantees in the Code are not backed by effective legal sanctions against non-compliance. The Code forbids the use of duress to extract information from a suspect or witness, but there is no clear rule excluding the use in court of evidence or testimony improperly obtained by the authorities. An accused may complain in court that a confession or testimony was extracted under duress, but the judge decides whether to admit the complaint as evidence.

Judges usually dismiss or ignore such pleas, and sometimes threaten defendants with legal action for perjury.

In addition, the judiciary's lack of independence means that judges are disinclined to pursue alleged breaches of the Code which emerge during a trial. Although the system of pre-trial hearings introduced in the 1981 Code should allow for some control in cases where torture has been used in investigations, judges are reluctant to rule against the police or other state authorities.

These problems are especially acute in the case of political detainees. Certain guarantees in the Code of Criminal Procedure do not apply to detainees accused of subversion. While the Code limits pre-trial detention, and requires judicial approval of detention beyond 60 days, the Anti-Subversion Law allows detention for periods of one year, renewable indefinitely on the authority of the Attorney General. In effect, this means that political suspects can be held indefinitely at the discretion of the local or regional military commander. The Code clearly states that only the police are authorized to carry out arrests and investigations, but in political cases military authorities assume these responsibilities. The Anti-Subversion Law also grants the security forces expanded powers of search and seizure, and imposes much heavier restrictions on detainees' access to legal assistance, relatives and doctors. In the rare event that an allegation of torture or ill-treatment is formally raised in court by a detainee, members of the judiciary tend to be even more reluctant than usual to take remedial action.

Human rights and impunity

In law the perpetrators of human rights violations can be brought to justice. Most of the acts that constitute or contribute to human rights violations are punishable under civil and military law. In practice, human rights abuses are seldom properly investigated, and few of those responsible are brought to justice. Members of the security forces are effectively granted immunity from punishment for wrongdoing. Existing procedures for seeking redress or compensation for the victims of human rights violations are also broadly ineffective.

The problem of impunity is most conspicuous where the suspected perpetrators are members of the military, and the victims are alleged government opponents. Only two soldiers have been convicted of a human rights offence in the past five years. Police

POWER AND IMPUNITY

Members of the military commit human rights violations with impunity. Even those responsible for gross abuses are seldom brought to justice. © *Steve Cox*

officers, prison officials, and police-trained security guards also commit violations with relative impunity. This contributes to, and helps to institutionalize, the cycle of human rights violations.

The story of Sofyan Lubis, a shoeshine boy aged 16, who died in the Tanjung Gusta Children's Prison in Medan in September 1992, is typical of many. Prison officials claimed that Sofyan Lubis suddenly became ill and died on the way to hospital. However, an autopsy concluded that his death had been "unnatural". Shortly after his death, prison officials tried to pre-empt legal action by asking his father to sign a statement promising not to file civil or criminal charges. He refused to do so. Sofyan's corpse bore clear signs of torture, according to relatives and lawyers; his stomach, chest and neck were severely bruised, two teeth were missing, and blood was coming from his mouth, nose, ears and genitals. A prisoner in a neighbouring cell said that she had heard screams coming from Sofyan's cell on the night of his death. A Ministry of Justice investigation concluded that Sofyan Lubis had not died of torture, but when challenged by doctors and relatives, the Ministry admitted its report was "not accurate". While the case remained in the public eye, government officials promised that it would be investigated thoroughly and that those responsible would be brought to justice. However, by mid-1994 no prison officer had been charged in connection with Sofyan Lubis's death.

The ineffectiveness of domestic mechanisms for bringing the perpetrators of human rights violations to justice highlights the importance of international standards and avenues for redress. Yet, despite its stated commitment to universal human rights standards, the Indonesian Government is not party to any of the major human rights treaties which proscribe serious human rights violations, such as the International Covenant on Civil and Political Rights (ICCPR) and the Convention against Torture and Other Cruel, Inhuman or Degrading Treatment or Punishment (CAT). Nor has it implemented the majority of UN recommendations on human rights in Indonesia and East Timor made since 1992.

Investigations

One of the primary causes of impunity in Indonesia is that investigations into alleged human rights violations are nearly always conducted by the security forces, and usually by members of the very unit believed to be responsible.

Even where investigations are formally handled by other government authorities, such as the Ministry of Justice or specially appointed commissions, the hand of the military is never far removed, and the results are much the same.

In most cases, military and government authorities respond to allegations of human rights abuse with a flat denial, pre-empting any investigation whatsoever. When the facts of abuse are irrefutable, the authorities attempt to justify them by invoking the interests of national security, stability and unity. Such statements often deflect demands for an inquiry; they also create a climate conducive to further violations. If a case of human rights abuse becomes the subject of intensive public complaint or of international scrutiny, military and police authorities generally give assurances that "appropriate measures" will be taken against the perpetrators if internal investigations reveal them to be at fault. Yet even in the most serious cases of abuse, they insist that the investigations must be conducted by military or police authorities, and that the findings need not be made public.

Strong domestic and international criticism sometimes results in investigations by other government authorities. However, these display many of the same defects as investigations by military and police officials. First, the lack of independence and impartiality of official investigations, and the fear of retribution, often inhibits witnesses from testifying openly. Second, the nature and conduct of the investigations usually remain obscure, so that there can be no independent verification of their findings. Third, when scrutinized these findings are often found to be false and aimed at whitewashing the role of the security forces. Fourth, official investigations into serious human rights violations almost always attempt to deflect attention from official responsibility by claiming the security forces were "provoked" by government opponents. Finally, the mandate and terms of reference of such investigations often prevent any discussion of the root causes of human rights violations.

Most of these shortcomings were highlighted by the official investigations of the Santa Cruz massacre of 12 November 1991 (see pages 50 to 54). Facing increasing international and domestic criticism, the government formed a National Commission of Inquiry to investigate the massacre. The commission's findings were released a month later. After examining that report, Amnesty International concluded that the commission's composition and methods of work were fatally flawed, and that many of its findings were unacceptable. The commission did not meet the criteria of independence, impartiality, and credibility required by the UN Principles for the Effective Prevention and Investigation of Extra-Legal, Arbitrary and Summary Executions. Members of the commission did not possess the technical expertise to conduct an investigation which required a thorough search for mass burial sites, full exhumations and the performance of autopsies. Most commission members had close links to the government or the military, and its interviews with eye-witnesses, most of them held in prison or military hospital, could not have been conducted confidentially. As a result most East Timorese were afraid to testify before the commission.

These problems were reflected in the commission's findings, which gave undue credence to military accounts of the incident while ignoring or misconstruing evidence, including eye-witness testimony, which contradicted the official version. Its report accused members of the funeral procession of "provoking" the massacre, while keeping criticism of the police and military to the barest minimum. The effect was to suggest that the peaceful expression of political dissent justified the use of lethal force or other unlawful measures against civilians. More than two years after the investigation, the government had yet to identify the vast majority of those killed; nor had it accounted for more than 200 people who "disappeared" after the massacre.

Punishment

Torture, murder and kidnapping are criminal offences under Indonesian law. They are also prohibited in the Military Penal Code and in a variety of ministerial regulations. Other provisions of the Military Code are designed to curtail the abuse of authority by members of the security forces and to ensure that commanding officers take responsibility for crimes committed by their subordinates. These laws and provisions could be used to prosecute those responsible for human rights violations as well as their commanding officers, but the political and legal obstacles any such action faces means that the perpetrators are seldom punished.

Army personnel and members of elite counter-insurgency units are the least likely to be prosecuted for human rights crimes. Police officers are marginally more likely to be tried and convicted, and generally receive light sentences. Those found guilty of torturing a prisoner to death have seldom been sentenced to more than three years' imprisonment; sentences of a few months are the norm. Heavier sentences are handed down to police auxiliaries and prison guards. This hierarchy of impunity mirrors the relative political power of the different services and units. It also reflects the fact that police auxiliaries and prison guards are tried in civilian courts, which are open to public scrutiny, while army and police personnel are tried in military courts, which are not.

On the few occasions when members of the security forces have been found responsible for serious violations, or where political pressure for government action has become insurmountable, they have been "disciplined". Disciplinary action can include demotion, transfer, dismissal, or the performance of military drill. Such punishments have been meted out in a few highly publicized recent cases. To the extent that such measures are virtually unprecedented, they could be seen as an improvement; some effort is being made to punish the perpetrators. Yet, in themselves such disciplinary measures are hardly sufficient. If they are used as a way of shielding the perpetrators from more serious punishment — as often appears to be the case — then they may actually contribute to the problem of impunity.

POWER AND IMPUNITY

Very few military or police personnel ever suffer more serious punishment, such as imprisonment. In fact, most cases never reach the trial stage, even where there is substantial evidence of responsibility. The government's lack of enthusiasm for punishing the perpetrators of human rights violations stands in marked contrast to the energy devoted to punishing political opponents.

Here again, the government's response to the Santa Cruz massacre is revealing. In early 1992 military authorities set up a Military Honour Council which was charged with investigating military responsibility. Following the recommendations of the Council, 10 members of the security forces were tried for disciplinary offences in June 1992, and a number of high-ranking officers were removed from their posts. This was an unprecedented move. Yet, despite as many as 270 killings and substantial evidence of torture during and after the massacre, none of those tried was charged with murder and only one, a police corporal, was charged with assault. All received sentences of between eight and 18 months' imprisonment. In contrast, East Timorese accused of organizing the peaceful procession were tried and sentenced to terms of up to life imprisonment after being convicted of subversion or other political crimes.

Given Indonesia's system of military justice, the infrequency of prosecutions for human rights crimes and the lightness of sentencing is not surprising. Military officers decide whether or not to proceed with a case, and criminal charges are heard before a military court. As with many military court systems, Indonesia's has a reputation for protecting members of the security forces who claim they were acting in the line of duty. Military court proceedings are closed to the public thereby removing a fundamental safeguard of judicial independence. Finally, the verdicts issued by military courts, if indeed they find the defendant guilty, are seldom made public, which diminishes their deterrent value.

Redress and compensation

Existing procedures for the redress and compensation of victims and relatives are ineffective and cumbersome. Members of the public with a human rights grievance face the daunting prospect of complaining to the very authorities they believe to be responsible. For most, particularly the economically disadvantaged or politically vulnerable, this is an insurmountable obstacle. Those who submit a complaint may face threats or physical violence from those they have accused. Only if families have the resolve and the financial means to push beyond this stage is there any chance of a fuller inquiry or legal proceedings.

Virtually the only institutional mechanism of bringing a complaint is the system of pre-trial hearings, introduced with the Code of Criminal Procedure in 1981. In theory, these hearings provide an opportunity for detainees to challenge the legality of arrest and interrogation procedures. Yet the system has so seldom resulted in a finding against the arresting authorities that even the most experienced lawyers regard it as a waste of time. Even when the courts have found against a member of the security forces, that decision has seldom had any effect on the outcome of the trial of the person wrongfully arrested or ill-treated.

The only alternative is for victims or their relatives to bring a civil suit for damages against members of the security forces or prison officials. This is an expensive, time consuming and onerous process and plaintiffs may face harassment and the threat of a counter-suit for damaging the reputation of the security forces. The final

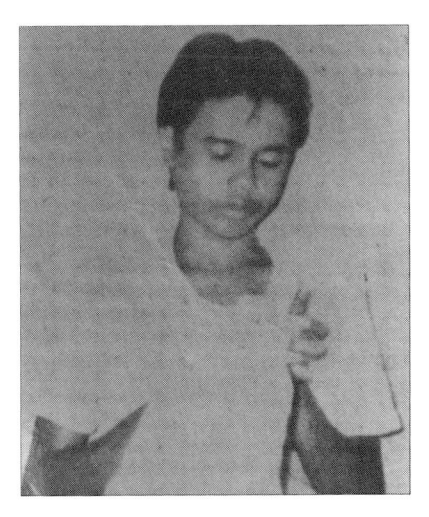

Leman was beaten to death by prison guards at Cipinang Prison, Jakarta, in 1986. Two guards found guilty of killing him were sentenced to short prison terms. His family brought a successful civil suit for damages and were awarded Rp 1 million, but had received no money by mid-1994.

injustice is that those who win such suits can wait years before receiving any compensation.

The shortcomings of the procedure are highlighted by the case of Leman, who was beaten to death by prison guards in 1986, while serving a six-month term for petty theft at Cipinang Prison, Jakarta. Leman's family initiated both a criminal case and a civil suit for damages. In August 1987 a court found two guards guilty of causing Leman's death but sentenced them to just a few months in jail. In December 1990, more than four years after the case had entered the courts, the Supreme Court found in favour of Leman's family, awarding them damages of Rp 1 million (about US$500). By mid-1994, they had yet to receive any money.

4

Extrajudicial execution

Arbitrary execution is an important element of the government's system of maintaining political "stability" and "order". Although especially common during counter-insurgency operations, extrajudicial executions are also a central component of the government's response to other perceived threats to national security, including peaceful protests, the establishment of "unorthodox" religious communities, and criminal activity.

Three basic types of extrajudicial killing are discernible in Indonesia and East Timor. First, there are deliberate secret killings of political prisoners in custody, sometimes after they have "disappeared". Second, there are killings which result from the deliberate use of excessive force in dealing with crowds or religious communities. Third, there are targeted "mysterious killings" by unidentified government death squads.

The precise techniques of killing differ somewhat according to the circumstances in which they occur. Deliberate killings in custody, following "disappearance", tend to occur where troops are engaged in counter-insurgency operations. Killings resulting from excessive use of force against crowds have more often occurred outside rebel areas. The technique of "mysterious killing" has been used with almost equal frequency both against alleged rebels and suspected criminals. The most striking aspect of extrajudicial executions in Indonesia and East Timor is the broad similarity of the techniques employed in different political contexts. This suggests that unlawful killing is a central aspect of government policy.

A similar uniformity marks the government's response to allegations of unlawful killings. The government has typically issued blanket denials of reports of extrajudicial executions and, with a few notable exceptions,

Protesters at the gateway to the Santa Cruz cemetery, Dili, shortly before soldiers opened fire, killing up to 270 people, on 12 November 1991.
© *Steve Cox*

has failed to conduct thorough and impartial investigations or to bring the perpetrators of such crimes to justice.

East Timor

As many as 270 civilians were killed on 12 November 1991, and immediately thereafter, when government troops opened fire on a peaceful procession at the Santa Cruz cemetery, in Dili. Most were shot while attempting to flee and others were beaten and stabbed. There were reports that dozens of people, including witnesses, were killed in the following weeks; some were recovering from their wounds in a military hospital.

The victims were among some 2,000 people who had joined a procession to the cemetery following a memorial mass for Sebastião Gomes, reportedly killed by Indonesian security forces on 28 October 1991. The shooting took place five to 10 minutes after the crowd had reached the cemetery. Some banners had been hung, people talked among themselves and a number shouted pro-independence slogans such as "Long live East Timor!". At

CHAPTER 4

that point, a large contingent of armed soldiers arrived, some on foot, others in vehicles.

Tension rose as the soldiers approached; people began to move away in fear. According to eye-witnesses, the foot soldiers marched to the entrance of the cemetery, formed a line about 12 men abreast, then opened fire on the crowd. No warning was given. Many of the dead were shot in the back.

The walls of the cemetery and the large number of people made it difficult to escape, but the shooting continued even as people tried to flee. An eye-witness said that minutes after the shooting began he saw about 100 bodies lying on the ground. Witnesses who had taken cover inside the cemetery said they saw soldiers beating wounded people with truncheons and the butts of their weapons. One foreigner, discovered by soldiers while hiding in the cemetery, said:

> *"I left the crypt with at least 10 people bleeding profusely and several dead. All the way to the entrance of the cemetery I was confronted by soldiers brandishing knives and thrusting them towards my face. I was kicked and beaten and had guns put to my head while they screamed at me."*

One of the dead was Domingos Segurado, who taught at the Portuguese language school in Dili. An activist in the underground resistance, he was one of the organizers of the protest, and had been in hiding for several weeks before. A reporter whom Domingos Segurado helped, remembers him as "an extremely gentle man... trying to bring about change in a non-violent way".

After the massacre, the bodies of the dead were loaded onto military trucks and buried in unmarked graves or dumped at sea. At least 91 of the wounded were taken to military hospital and an estimated 300 people were arrested in mopping-up operations. There were credible reports that some of those in hospital were ill-treated, and that some were deliberately "finished off". Military authorities prevented relatives, the UN Special Rapporteur on torture and representatives of the International Committee of the Red Cross (ICRC) from visiting those in prison and hospital.

There were unconfirmed reports that another 60 to 80 people were killed on 15 November, and their bodies buried in large unmarked graves outside Dili. According to these reports, the victims were taken in military trucks from various prisons in Dili

POWER AND IMPUNITY

Preparing for the march to the Santa Cruz cemetery. The slogans read: "Out with the invaders... no to integration". © *Steve Cox*

CHAPTER 4

Some of the wounded sheltering in a chapel during the Santa Cruz massacre. The government has failed to account for the dead and the "disappeared". It is believed many bodies were disposed of secretly. © *Steve Cox*

to a place on the outskirts of town. Before being loaded onto the trucks, the prisoners were reportedly made to strip naked, blindfolded and had their hands tied behind their backs. They were reportedly taken to the edge of newly dug ditches and shot with automatic weapons.

Facing a storm of local and international protest, Indonesian government and military authorities expressed regret at the loss of life at Santa Cruz and promised a prompt investigation (see pages 44 to 45). However, from the outset, they attempted to justify the action of the security forces and to place responsibility for the massacre on the mourners themselves. Military authorities claimed that soldiers had been forced to shoot when "the mob attacked them brutally". Such claims were at odds with eye-witness testimony, and other evidence including film footage, that the procession was peaceful and that the soldiers fired without warning and without provocation. Some military officials took a more bellicose stance. One day after the massacre, the Commander of the Armed Forces (now Vice-President), General Try Sutrisno, said that people in the procession had "spread chaos" by unfurling posters with slogans discrediting the government, and by shouting "many unacceptable things". In response, he said, the soldiers had fired shots into the air, "...but they persisted with their misdeeds...In the end, they had to be shot. These ill-bred people have to be shot...and we will shoot them".

Aceh

Some 2,000 civilians, including children and the very elderly, were killed by Indonesian soldiers in or near the province of Aceh between 1989 and 1993. Some died in public executions; others were killed secretly and their often mutilated bodies were left in public places. Scores of the dead were dumped in mass graves. The timing of the killings, the methods and techniques employed, and the public comments made by military officers in the region, strongly suggest that extrajudicial execution was a deliberate part of counter-insurgency strategy. By mid-1994 the authorities had not initiated any investigation into the killings, and no member of the security forces had been punished.

Summary or arbitrary executions by government forces were initially reported in 1989, shortly after the first *Aceh Merdeka* attacks, and intermittent reports continued through the first half of 1990. However, extrajudicial executions on a mass scale appear to have begun in July 1990, immediately after the President ordered the deployment of some 6,000 counter-insurgency troops. This was also the point at which the pattern of "mysterious killings", responsible for hundreds of civilian deaths, began to emerge.

The "mysterious killings" in Aceh had the following general features. The corpses of victims were usually left in public places, apparently as a warning to others not to join or support the rebels. Most had clearly been prisoners when they were killed. Their thumbs, and sometimes their feet, had been tied together with a particular type of knot. Most had been shot at close range, though the bullets were seldom found in their bodies. Most also showed signs of having been beaten with a blunt instrument or tortured, and their faces were often unrecognizable. Most of the bodies were not recovered by relatives or friends, both out of fear of retribution by the military and because the victims were usually dumped some distance from their home villages.

One of the victims was Teungku Ahmad Lutan, a suspected *Aceh Merdeka* supporter. He was tortured and killed in military custody in May 1990. According to eye-witnesses, soldiers of Battalion 111 arrested Teungku Ahmad Lutan in Idi Cut, Peureulak, and took him to their camp in nearby Tualang Cut for interrogation. Three days later his mutilated body was dumped in a ditch near his home. When local residents found him, his hands were tied behind his back, his head was smashed, and his body bore signs of torture. His relatives were afraid to pick up the body for fear of retribution from the military. When other villagers went to retrieve the corpse, they were confronted by soldiers who demanded: "What do you think you're doing burying him? Don't you know he's a rebel?".

Most victims of extrajudicial execution were villagers living in areas of suspected rebel activity. One objective of the killings was apparently to terrorize the local population so that they would cooperate with the security forces in tracking down alleged rebels. However, some villagers were killed in reprisal for the death of a soldier, or for failing promptly to obey a military command. When soldiers were unable to find or kill a rebel suspect, they often took revenge on their friends or close relatives.

Djamilah Abubakar, aged 24 and the wife of a suspected *Aceh Merdeka* member, was shot dead in military custody in March 1991. Djamilah's encounters with the military began in mid-June 1989, when dozens of soldiers came to the family home searching for her husband, a fisherman named Mohammad Jasin bin Pawang Piah. When she told the soldiers that he was at sea and would be gone for several days, they shouted "You're lying!". They forced her at gunpoint to admit that her husband was an *Aceh Merdeka* member. One soldier then ordered her to undress, and jabbed her body with his rifle. When Jasin returned home several days later, he found his house burned to the ground and learned that Djamilah had gone to another village to stay with relatives. She remained there for about six months, until soldiers came to that area warning villagers not to give shelter to those linked with *Aceh Merdeka*, and mentioning her by name as a suspect. In early 1990 she fled to another village and remained there for about a year. However, on about 24 March 1991, shortly after Jasin had visited her, she was arrested by soldiers. Two days later her corpse was found by the roadside in a village some 15 kilometres away. Her head was smashed and she had been shot in the chest.

Not all victims of unlawful killing in Aceh were left in public places. Many were thrown into mass graves, some of which reportedly contained hundreds of bodies. According to one report, a group of 56 detainees were summarily executed by Indonesian troops on 12 September 1990 at Bukit Panglima, on the road between Bireuen and Takengon. Witnesses said the detainees were ordered off the military trucks in which they were being transported, lined up on the edge of a ravine, and shot. According to another report, a mass grave containing some 200 bodies was discovered near the village of Alue Mira in mid-1990. The Regional Military Commander disputed the number of corpses but did not deny the existence of the grave. In November 1990 he told a journalist:

"The grave certainly exists but I don't think it could have been 200 bodies. It's hard to tell with arms and heads all mixed up."[15]

While they have formally denied responsibility for arbitrary killings, government and military authorities have made public statements which condone and even encourage the use of extrajudicial execution in counter-insurgency operations. In May 1990 General Try Sutrisno admitted military responsibility for some "accidental" civilian deaths in Aceh, but attempted to justify them by saying: "If there were victims on the civilian side, that was something that could not be avoided."[16] Commenting on the public display of corpses, six months later, a military officer in Aceh said: "Okay, that does happen. But the rebels use terrorist strategies so we are forced to use anti-terrorist strategies."[17] Asked whether the "mysterious killings" were intended as "shock therapy", the Regional Military Commander, Major General H.R. Pramono, replied:

"As a strategy, that's true. But our goal is not bad...We only kill them if they are [Aceh Merdeka] *members."*[18]

The scale of killing in Aceh has diminished since late 1991. With the arrest, death or flight of *Aceh Merdeka's* field commanders, there is no military or political rationale for continued extrajudicial executions. However, there has been no fundamental change in the counter-insurgency strategy employed by the Indonesian armed forces, a central component of which is the killing of civilians in guerrilla base areas. If *Aceh Merdeka* were to increase its activities, the pattern of political killings would probably re-emerge almost immediately. Just as importantly, the fate of most of those killed in past years has yet to be clarified, there have been no investigations into the killings, and no official condemnation of the practice.

Irian Jaya

Hundreds of real or suspected supporters of independence in Irian Jaya have been killed by Indonesian forces conducting counter-insurgency operations in the territory. Many of the victims were OPM fighters killed in combat, but some OPM fighters were deliberately killed in military custody, while other victims were civilians.

In 1990 government security forces reportedly shot and beheaded a man they suspected of OPM membership. Eye-witnesses said that soldiers shot Soleman Daundi shortly after he surrendered to local authorities in Napdari village in May 1990. The soldiers reportedly cut off his head and took it to the local military headquarters at Wardo, displaying it in more than a dozen villages along the way. According to reports, Soleman Daundi's head was also shown to military officers at the Military Resort Command (KOREM 173) and the Military District Command (KODIM 1708). It was then handed over to a priest in Wardo and buried. Soleman Daundi had apparently been involved in a pro-independence flag-raising ceremony in Sopen in December 1989 and had subsequently gone into hiding.

Despite restrictions on access to Irian Jaya by independent observers, Amnesty International has continued to receive credible reports of such killings in recent years, many of them along the Indonesia-Papua New Guinea border. Thirteen people were reportedly killed and eight wounded by Indonesian soldiers in October 1993 in Yapsie village, approximately 12 kilometres inside Papua New Guinea. Those reportedly killed were named as: Adolf Tablop, Betimeus Tablop, Dariana Hawngap, Diman Kakadi, Januarius Hawngap, Junus Tablop, Matina Tablop, Mayana Hawngap, Obeth Tablop, Okbom Tablop, Philipus Hawngap, Pius Kalamabin and Susana Bawi. Eye-witnesses said that the soldiers surrounded the village and opened fire. Among those seriously wounded in the attack were Naok Naplo, who was said to have been bayoneted in the neck, and Robert Tablo, who had two fingers shot from his hand. These injuries were said to have been inflicted after the two men had raised their hands in surrender.

Peaceful protesters

Government forces have killed hundreds of civilians in areas of relative political stability, including the islands of Java and Sumatra and the capital city, Jakarta. In 1993 the victims included four villagers peacefully protesting against eviction from their land; four members of a religious community thought to pose a challenge to government authority; and a worker involved in a peaceful industrial dispute.

The killings of peaceful demonstrators and attacks on vulnerable communities reveal certain similarities in the behaviour and the attitudes of the security forces. There is the tradition of political repression, characterized by intolerance of political opposition before overt force is used. There is a pattern in official justifications for such killings, typified by attempts to accuse the victims of provoking government forces. Finally, there is the routine failure to conduct thorough and impartial investigations and to bring the perpetrators to justice.

The Nipah dam killings

Four people were killed and three others injured when security forces opened fire on some 500 peaceful demonstrators at the proposed site of the Nipah dam on the island of Madura on 25 September 1993. They were protesting against the construction of the dam, which would flood their land and submerge four villages. Those killed were Mutirah, a mother of three aged 51, a 14-year-old schoolboy named Nindin bin Musa, a 28-year-old man named Samuki P. Supriadi, and another man, Muhammad, who died five days later of his injuries.

According to independent sources, the killings occurred as villagers, many of them women and children, approached a team of government surveyors, accompanied by at least 20 police and military personnel, to voice their opposition to the project. The shooting reportedly began on orders from the commander of the Banyuates Sub-District Military Command (KORAMIL). A fact-finding mission by the Indonesian Legal Aid Foundation (LBH) found no evidence that the demonstrators had carried any weapons or that they had behaved in an aggressive or threatening manner.

CHAPTER 4

A local man holds some of the bullets found after security forces opened fire on a peaceful demonstration against the construction of the Nipah dam in September 1993. Four people were killed and three others injured. The dam project will submerge four villages. © *Tempo*

The mission concluded that the demonstration was peaceful and that the security forces had opened fire without warning or provocation.

The day before the killings the government team, accompanied by police and military personnel, had gone to the area to survey the site. Local people protested to the team that no agreement had been reached between the local residents and the authorities. Before leaving the site, a member of the security forces reportedly threatened the villagers by saying: "When we begin work tomorrow, nobody must leave their homes...or they will be shot!" The government official responsible for the project, the *Bupati* of Sampang, had reportedly issued similar threats in previous weeks and had accused protestors of being PKI members. At a meeting with villagers on 11 August 1993, he said: "I will arrest anyone who prevents the construction of this dam. I'm in charge of security. I have the armed forces. All I have to do is give the order".[19]

Following protests from local religious and community leaders, in October the armed forces commander, General Feisal Tanjung, announced that an internal inquiry into the incident had been ordered and that those found guilty would be punished. Shortly thereafter two police and two military officers were transferred from their posts. However, by mid-1994, no member of the security forces had been charged with human rights-related offences or punished in connection with the killings. Government and military authorities insisted that there was no need for an independent investigation. Despite demands from religious and community leaders and human rights organizations, the government refused to take action against the civilian officials with overall responsibility, both of whom were former military officers.

The *Haur Koneng* killings

Four members of a small and isolated religious community in West Java, including a 12-year-old boy, were shot and killed on 29 July 1993 when government forces stormed their meeting place in Sinargalih, a village in the district of Majalengka. Two members of the group (known as *Haur Koneng*, Yellow Bamboo), Jaenuddin and Ahmad, were killed outright; the group's leader, Abdul Manan, and another man, Wahyudin, died in hospital in the following days. Abdul Manan had been shot five times in the stomach at close range. At least 10 others, including four children, were injured in the raid, six of them seriously. Nineteen people, including the injured, were arrested; their trials began in October 1993.

According to reports, eight police and three Mobile Brigade members first went to the group's headquarters on 28 June to arrest three members of the sect who had been accused of punching the village head in a dispute over land. A struggle ensued, during which one man was shot and the local chief of police was stabbed and killed. The next morning, a joint force of more than 100 police, army troops of Battalion 321 and Mobile Brigades, arrived in the village. The police claimed that Abdul Manan and the others were shot and killed as he and 18 followers tried to resist arrest. However, eye-witnesses said the troops attacked without provocation, launching grenades and tear-gas into the small compound, and then shooting at the occupants as they fled the burning buildings. Witnesses also said that the security forces had delayed taking the wounded to hospital, leaving them lying in the yard of a local rice mill for nearly three hours. According to medical professionals,

CHAPTER 4

police authorities had obstructed their efforts to treat Abdul Manan and eight others. Military and police authorities also prevented victims from meeting relatives or human rights lawyers, and obstructed efforts by independent organizations to conduct investigations.

Government officials tried to justify the attack by claiming that the *Haur Koneng* group posed a threat to security and stability, and that its members had refused to take part in local or national elections, to carry official identity cards or to send their children to government schools.

However, domestic human rights organizations which conducted independent investigations into the assault concluded that the security forces had used excessive force and had deliberately killed unarmed civilians. Religious and community leaders, and local members of the legislative assembly, criticized the tactics used against a small, unarmed religious community. Government and military officials defended the use of "firm measures" as necessary for the maintenance of law and order.

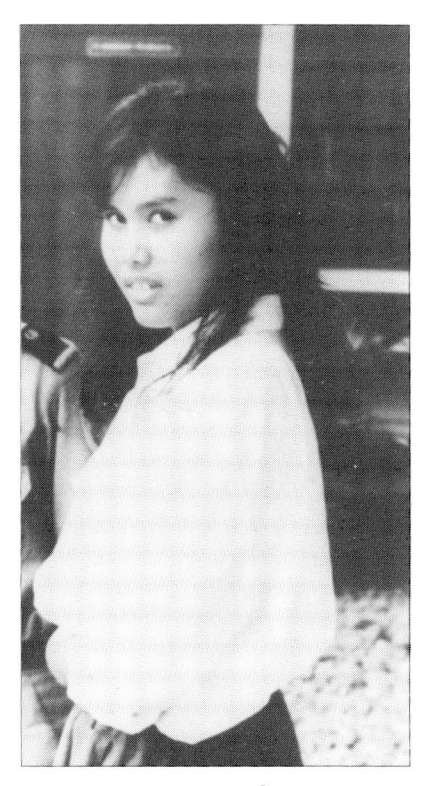

Wawat Setiawati, aged 18, was one of three female members of a small religious community in West Java who were jailed because they had prayed rather than surrender to the police. Four members of the community, including a 12-year-old boy, were killed when police stormed their meeting place in July 1993.
© *Yayasan Pijar*

61

POWER AND IMPUNITY

In response to public pressure, the police initiated an investigation, but the government refused to conduct an independent public inquiry. No member of the security forces had been charged in connection with the killings by mid-1994 and there was no indication that any would be.

In marked contrast, by the end of 1993 at least eight *Haur Koneng* members had been tried on various charges, and sentenced to jail terms of between four months and one year. They included three young women accused of failing to obey police orders to surrender during the assault. In his summing up, the judge said that, rather than surrendering, the three women had "...gathered together and chanted prayers until the clash between the police officers and the sect's followers occurred".[20]

The killing of Marsinah

Marsinah, a factory worker aged 25, was "disappeared", tortured, raped and killed in East Java in early May 1993 because of her role as a labour activist. The circumstances of her "disappearance" and death, and of the official investigation that followed, strongly suggest that her killing was planned and carried out with the knowledge and acquiescence of military authorities.

Marsinah was found dead in a shack at the edge of a field about 200 kilometres from her home in Porong, East Java, on 8 May. Her body was bloodied and covered in bruises, and her neck bore the marks of strangulation. An autopsy revealed that her attackers had thrust a blunt instrument into her vagina causing severe bleeding.

In the days before her death, Marsinah had been actively involved in a strike at the watch factory. Military authorities, including the Commanders of the District Military Command (KODIM) and the Sub-District Military Command (KORAMIL), had intervened directly in the dispute and interrogated the workers about their role in the strike. On 5 May, 13 workers were summoned by the military and given the choice of resigning or facing charges for holding "illegal meetings" or "inciting" others to strike. During the interrogations, some workers were beaten and one was threatened with death. That evening Marsinah went to the local military headquarters to look for her colleagues. She then "disappeared" until her body was found three days later. Pressure from labour activists and human rights groups forced the police to open an investigation, but it was swiftly taken over by military intelligence authorities. At the outset the authorities strenuously denied that

CHAPTER 4

Marsinah's death was related to the labour dispute, and attempted to play down all evidence of military involvement. However, in November 1993, nine civilians, all of them company staff or executives, and one military officer, the KORAMIL Commander, were charged in connection with the murder and brought to trial. Extreme irregularities in the arrest, investigation and trial procedures — which violated both international law and Indonesia's Code of Criminal Procedure — suggested that the trials were intended to obscure military responsibility for the killing.

Several of the accused, including one woman, were kidnapped by military intelligence officers in early October, held incommunicado for up to three weeks, and forced to confess to the murder, some of them under torture. During the trials, all nine civilian defendants retracted their interrogation statements, saying that they had been extracted under duress or torture. In March 1944 the National Human Rights Commission confirmed that some of the defendants had been tortured and that the basic rights of all had been violated by the military

Marsinah, a 25-year-old factory worker, was apparently killed by the military because she was a trade union activist.

63

authorities. Nevertheless, the trials proceeded, and by May 1994, four of the defendants had been convicted, three of them receiving sentences of 12 years' imprisonment. The sole military officer arrested, the KORAMIL Commander, was charged only with a disciplinary offence for failing to report a crime.

Following months of independent investigation with other non-governmental organizations, the LBH concluded in March 1994 that there was a strong possibility that Marsinah had been killed in the KODIM headquarters, and that ultimate responsibility for the murder rested with higher ranking military authorities. Even the National Human Rights Commission suggested that "other parties" may have been involved in Marsinah's murder. However, neither the LBH nor the Human Rights Commission had the authority to bring criminal charges against the suspected perpetrators, who remained beyond the reach of the law.

Criminal suspects

Thousands of real or alleged criminals have been deliberately killed by the security forces, or by death squads operating on government orders. These assassinations reached a peak in the mid-1980s, but have continued on a reduced scale in recent years. In response to criticism, the authorities have defended their actions as necessary to fight crime. In early 1994, the Commander of *Kopassus* asked: "Which is more important? Protecting the human rights of criminals or those of the good guys?".

Between 1983 and 1986, government death squads summarily executed an estimated 5,000 alleged criminals in various cities in Indonesia. These "mysterious killings" were carried out by squads of men in plain clothes driving unmarked vehicles. The authorities denied any responsibility for the killings, blaming the deaths on gang warfare. However, in 1989 President Suharto revealed in his memoirs that the "mysterious killings" had been carried out by members of the security forces and represented a deliberate government policy to deal with "criminal elements" through a kind of public "shock therapy":

> "*Those who tried to resist, like it or not, had to be shot....Some of the corpses were left [in public places]...for the purpose of* shock therapy....*This was done so that the general public would understand that there was still*

CHAPTER 4

someone capable of taking action to tackle the problem of criminality."[21]

The "mysterious killings" campaign drew to a close in 1986, but the idea behind it remained. When confronted by evidence of rising criminality, police and military authorities still resort to summary measures. In Jakarta a "shoot-on-sight" policy instituted by the police chief in 1989 left at least 200 dead over four years. Many of the victims died in suspicious circumstances in police custody. In most cases, police authorities claimed the victim was shot while trying to escape. However, the circumstances of the killings cast serious doubt on such claims.

On 24 May 1993 Hartono, a suspected thief, was shot dead while allegedly trying to flee police custody. He was wearing handcuffs when he was shot. According to official sources, the police had taken Hartono to West Jakarta to identify the hide-out of a member of his criminal gang. A police spokesperson said that as they walked towards the hideout, Hartono suddenly "...tried to run away and free his hands from the hand-cuffs. The officers said he broke the hand-cuffs".[22] The officers involved claimed that because Hartono had ignored three police warnings they were "forced to shoot him". No further investigation was known to have been undertaken by mid-1994 and no police officers had been brought to justice.

The summary execution of suspected criminals is also commonplace outside Jakarta. Syamsul Bahri died on 16 June 1993 after being beaten and shot several times in the custody of police from Pangkalanbrandan, North Sumatra. According to the police, Syamsul Bahri was shot twice in the legs because he tried to resist arrest and threatened the five armed police officers with a machete. The police claimed that he bled to death on the way to hospital. However, relatives said that there were several bullet wounds in Syamsul Bahri's chest, and signs that he had been beaten before he died. Eye-witnesses denied that he had confronted police with a machete and said that, after being shot in the legs, he had been taken to a cemetery. Local residents testified that shortly thereafter eight gunshots were heard in the cemetery. Police investigations confirmed that Syamsul Bahri had been badly beaten and that there were several bullet wounds in his body. Relatives and neighbours complained to the Pangkalanbrandan police chief, who promised that "...any police officer found guilty would be dealt with in accordance with the law".[23] The Chief of Police for North Sumatra

POWER AND IMPUNITY

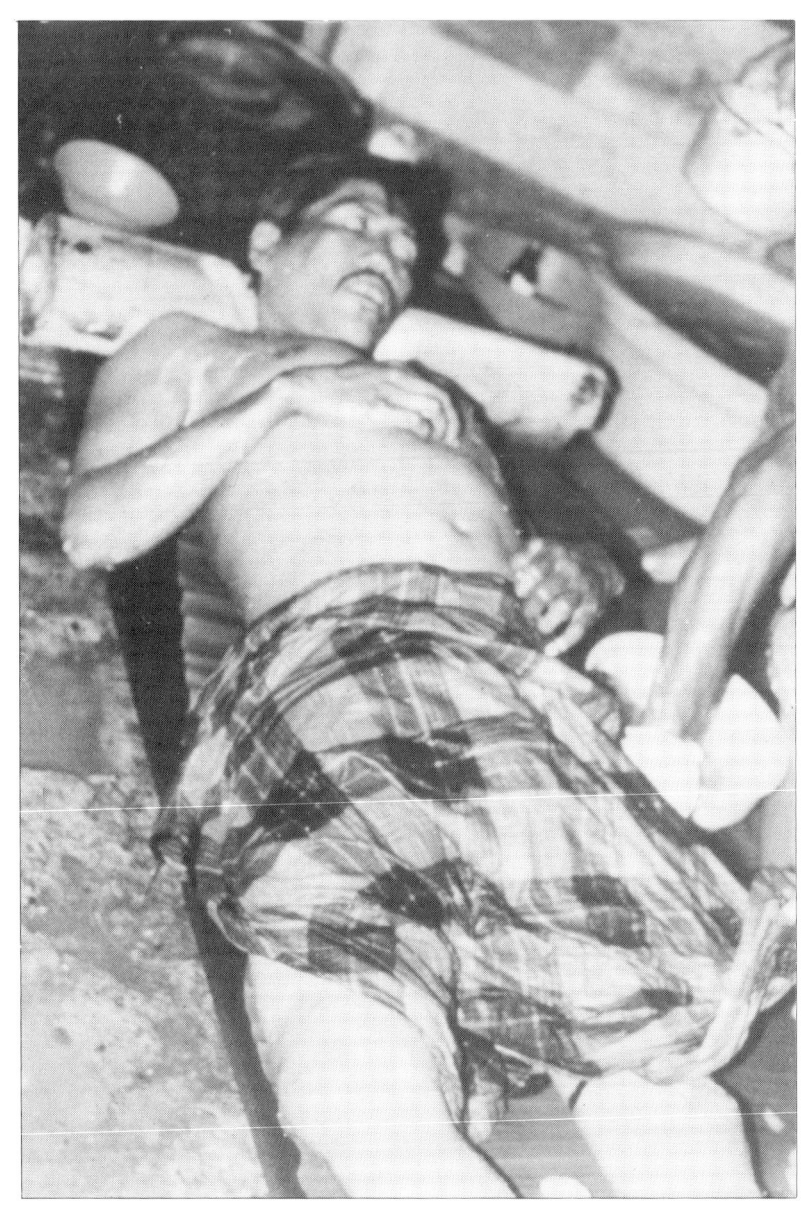

Syamsul Bahri, aged 35, died in police custody in North Sumatra in June 1993. A suspected criminal, he had been beaten and shot several times. None of the officers involved have been brought to justice.

said in July that the police officers were being questioned, but there was no indication that any of them had been charged or tried by mid-1994.

The rate of summary killings has continued to increase in recent years. According to the LBH, 134 suspected criminals were shot and killed by police in Greater Jakarta between 1992 and early 1994. In April 1994 the authorities announced that 16,700 soldiers and police had been mobilized to conduct a new anti-crime drive, called "Operation Cleansing", in order to clear the city of criminals before the November APEC summit. Before the end of the April, some 700 suspects had been detained and three had been shot dead, one of them while in handcuffs. The campaign has been enthusiastically endorsed by high-ranking police and military authorities. In April 1994, Jakarta's Police Chief, Major General Hindarto said:

"Jakarta must be cleared of all criminals... Educating them is no longer an effective means of bringing down the rate of...violent crime here...We have no choice but to impose harsh laws."[24]

5

Torture, ill-treatment and death in custody

Torture and ill-treatment are prohibited under the Indonesian Criminal Code, the Code of Criminal Procedure and by various ministerial regulations. According to the authorities, they are also proscribed by armed forces service oaths. However, these laws and regulations have not prevented torture and ill-treatment, or provided effective avenues for redress. Nor have they been effective in ensuring that the perpetrators are brought promptly to justice.

Torture and ill-treatment is commonplace in Indonesia and East Timor and regularly results in death or serious injury. Whether the victims are political or criminal suspects, there appears to be a standard set of methods of torture and ill-treatment. While this does not prove that torture is overt government policy, it does indicate that the practice of torture has become institutionalized within the security forces.

A military manual issued to troops in East Timor in the early 1980s substantiates this view, at least in relation to counter-insurgency operations. One passage from the manual reads:

"It is hoped that interrogation with the use of force will not be implemented except in those situations where the person examined tells the truth with difficulty. However, if the use of force is required...the local population...should not...witness it, in order to avoid arousing the antipathy of the people....Avoid taking photographs showing torture (of someone being given electric shocks, stripped naked and so on)...." [25]

People arrested during counter-insurgency operations, whether in East Timor or in Indonesia, continue to be especially vulnerable to torture. But they are not alone. Members of poor communities resisting eviction, striking workers, student demonstrators and journalists are often ill-treated and sometimes tortured in custody, particularly if they have been detained by military personnel. Criminal suspects and prisoners, particularly the poor and socially disadvantaged, are frequently ill-treated and tortured and some have died or suffered serious injury as a result.

Recent evidence provided by the testimony of torture victims indicates that torture techniques have become standardized. Most political detainees experience some or all of the following methods: beating on the head, shins and torso with fists, lengths of wood, iron bars, bottles, rocks or electric cables; burning with lighted cigarettes; electrocution; slashing with razor blades and knives; death threats, mock executions and deliberate wounding with firearms; immersion for long periods in fetid water; suspension upside-down by the ankles; isolation, sleep and food deprivation; mutilation of the genitals, sexual molestation and rape.

During counter-insurgency operations torture is used to obtain political and military intelligence, to extract confessions for use in political trials and to intimidate local communities. Some instances of torture and ill-treatment may be the result of indiscipline on the part of ordinary soldiers, but torture appears to be used primarily to obtain information and instil fear.

Relatives and friends of suspected rebels have been tortured and ill-treated to extract information from them, to force them to cooperate in locating suspects or to put pressure on a suspect to surrender. Security forces have also ill-treated and tortured civilians living in areas thought to be sympathetic to the rebels. These actions have taken the form of threats, beatings, night-time house raids, house-burnings, forced patrols and occasionally rape.

East Timor

Since the invasion of 1975, real and suspected supporters of independence for East Timor have been routinely ill-treated and tortured by Indonesian military personnel. Torture has been facilitated by the practice of unacknowledged, arbitrary detention, by the existence of numerous secret detention centres and by the virtual autonomy granted to the military in East Timor to crush all opposition. Speaking to a journalist in April 1993, the head of the Catholic Church in East Timor, Bishop Belo, said that political prisoners there are tortured "just like two plus two equals four".

POWER AND IMPUNITY

In his January 1992 report the UN Special Rapporteur on torture concluded that torture was common in East Timor, and offered 11 concrete recommendations to prevent it. In 1992 and again in 1993 the UN Commission on Human Rights urged the government to implement these recommendations. The government promised to do so but, by mid-1994, it had begun to implement only one of them, with the formation of a National Human Rights Commission.

An East Timorese youth arrested in September 1992, eight months after the UN appeal, gave the following account of his treatment in custody:

> "*I was accused of being the leader of the clandestine group...Since I denied this, they began again with their dreadful torture: electric shocks, beatings with a club and, while forced to kneel on sharp rocks, I was burned with cigarettes and electric irons. Today my whole body bears the scars resulting from this torture.*
>
> "*During the interrogations one of my colleagues...was also brought in and subjected to torture. When I first saw him, I was totally unable to recognize him because of the physical state he was in.*"

Torture has sometimes resulted in hospitalization and death. Two youths, among 20 students arrested during a military operation in Baucau district in December 1992, reportedly died as a result of torture. Adelino Gomes Fonsesca was one of them. After being interrogated he was returned to a room where another student was being held. He had been badly beaten, was bleeding and his eyes were so swollen he could barely open them. He was suffering from severe pains in his chest and was breathing with difficulty. He died in the early hours of 25 December.

Torture and ill-treatment in East Timor is not confined to those suspected of political opposition. The relatives of real or suspected political opponents — including young girls and elderly men and women — have also been subjected to torture and ill-treatment, including rape, in an effort to obtain information on the whereabouts or activities of their relatives, or to force those being sought to give themselves up.

One woman and her family suffered several days of torture in Baucau by soldiers searching for her son whom they suspected of membership of a pro-independence group. The woman was arrested on 8 September 1992 and interrogated. When she denied knowing where her son was, she was stripped naked, beaten and kicked and given electric shocks. Three days after her arrest, one of her nephews and her sister-in-law were called in for questioning and were also tortured. The 19-year-old nephew was beaten, kicked and given electric shocks; he was stripped naked, lighted cigarettes were applied to his genitals and his pubic hair was set alight. The sister-in-law was beaten, kicked, stripped naked and tortured with electric shocks, and repeatedly sexually abused by soldiers during her five days in detention.

The Indonesian authorities have consistently denied allegations of ill-treatment and torture in East Timor, and have instead questioned the political motives of those who have reported them. The authorities have sometimes promised to investigate reports of torture, but have seldom actually done so.

Aceh

Torture has been used routinely in Aceh since mid-1989, and in a number of cases it has resulted in death. Incidents of torture and ill-treatment have been reported at virtually every level of the military command structure and in dozens of security force installations. Suspected rebels arrested in Aceh have also been tortured in military and police installations in the neighbouring province of North Sumatra.

Adnan Beuransyah, a journalist with the newspaper *Serambi Indonesia* and a lecturer at the National Islamic Institute, was arrested in August 1990 and held incommunicado for nearly eight months before being brought to trial. He was convicted of subversion and sentenced to eight years' imprisonment in May 1991, despite evidence that his confession of links to *Aceh Merdeka* had been extracted under torture. His sentence was increased to nine years in July 1991 following an appeal to the Aceh High Court. In his defence plea he described his treatment while detained by soldiers of the Resort Military Command (KOREM/012) post at Lampineung, Banda Aceh:

> "*I was stripped to my underwear and my hands were handcuffed behind me. Then I was kicked and punched about the chest and legs until I fell on the floor. I was forced into consciousness again only to be kicked and punched all over my body. I collapsed again and had difficulty breathing. This went on for about an hour. Then I was taken*

> to another room....I was hit with a block of wood and beaten and kicked.
>
> "My shins were a particular target, and I still bear the scars on my back. My hair and nose were burned with cigarette butts. I was given electric shocks on my feet, genitals and ears until I fainted. Then I was ordered to sit with my legs outstretched and a length of wood was held down over my knees. Another length was placed under my buttocks which was then pumped up and down like someone jacking up a car. My knees felt as though they would break.
>
> "In this position I was ordered to confess to all the accusations against me. I thought then, it's better to admit to anything they want. The pumping ceased...I was still blindfolded and the wire for electric shocks was still wound around my big toes. If I said anything they didn't like, they'd turn on the current....It continued like this until I signed the interrogation deposition."

Responding to an enquiry from the UN Special Rapporteur on torture, dated 21 August 1992, the government acknowledged that Adnan Beuransyah had been arrested and tried, but said there was "no indication whatsoever" that he had been tortured.[26]

The families of suspected rebels in Aceh have also been tortured and ill-treated. Nasrun Majid was arrested in June 1990 when some 40 soldiers came to his family's house in Alue Nirih, Peureulak. They were searching for his elder brother, Razali Abdul Hamid, a suspected *Aceh Merdeka* activist. Nasrun Majid was held for 11 days at the KODIM in Lhokseumawe. According to relatives, he was beaten on the shins and head with a wooden club while being questioned. He was released on condition that he help to turn his brother over to the authorities. Razali's wife was also pressured to reveal information about his whereabouts. Towards the end of 1990, soldiers went to her house in Alue Nirih to find out where he was. When she said that she did not know, a soldier reportedly grabbed her new-born baby and, holding it upside-down, said: "If we can't get your husband we'll take the baby instead!". Eventually the soldiers departed, leaving the baby behind, but for about six months afterwards soldiers visited the house at least once a week. In March 1991, 17 members of the family decided to seek asylum in Malaysia, where they were detained as illegal immigrants.

CHAPTER 5

Irian Jaya

In July 1990, a suspected OPM leader named Melkianus Salosa was forcibly returned to Indonesia from Papua New Guinea. On arrival he was immediately arrested and placed in incommunicado military custody. He was convicted of subversion and sentenced to life imprisonment in March 1991. A few months after his arrest, reports emerged that he had been tortured. According to one report, Salosa's fingernails and toenails had been extracted, several of his teeth had been knocked out, and he had sustained serious bruising to the face. A political prisoner held in the same prison, but later released, claimed to have seen Salosa being taken from his cell bleeding heavily from the hands. About one year later, Melkianus Salosa was found dead outside the high security prison where he had been detained. Military authorities claimed he had escaped and died of exposure, but available evidence suggested that he had been deliberately killed in military custody.

Peaceful protesters

Ill-treatment is a hallmark of the government's response to peaceful political protest or perceived threats to "public order", inflicted as punishment for exercising the freedoms of speech and association which are, in principle, guaranteed by the Constitution. The victims have included demonstrators, workers on strike, human rights activists and university students, as well as people threatened with eviction from their homes. Members of poor communities have also been ill-treated by security personnel carrying out so-called "cleanliness" and "order" campaigns. Journalists and photographers reporting demonstrations or the activities of the security forces have also been ill-treated.

The ill-treatment of such groups often entails beating, kicking and threats. When protesters or suspected political opponents are detained for questioning, more severe forms of torture, including electric shocks and rape, are not uncommon.

At least 17 students, including one woman, were tortured or ill-treated while being interrogated by military intelligence authorities in Surabaya, East Java, on 25 and 26 January 1993. The students had joined a peaceful protest in support of farmers from Belangguan, who had been forced off their land to make way for military training facilities. The students were forced to strip, hit with metal rods and punched in the face and the stomach. At least 11 of them were tortured with electric shocks.

Three young factory workers — a man named Imam Basuki and two women known as "Das" and "Mep" — were reportedly tortured or ill-treated while held incommunicado for three days at the Resort Military Command (KOREM) in Surabaya, East Java, in January 1993. Imam Basuki was beaten until his face was badly swollen and "Das" was raped. The three workers, who had been active in a protracted labour dispute at the PT Victory Long Age factory, were abducted by soldiers in December 1992 and taken to the headquarters of KOREM 084/Bhaskara Jaya. The two women said they were taken to a separate room, but could hear Imam Basuki crying out as he was beaten. The following morning two soldiers entered the women's room and raped "Das". She was raped again twice by another soldier who reportedly boasted: "Go ahead and report us to [the commander]. He's not going to do a thing. This is our right!". The three were released only after they had signed statements that they would not complain about their treatment, and promising to take no part in further industrial action.

Criminal suspects and prisoners

Criminal suspects are tortured and ill-treated by police and prison officials throughout Indonesia and East Timor. The methods commonly reported include: beatings with batons, metal bars, lengths of electric cable and fists. Sexual molestation and rape have also been reported. Police and prison officers sometimes inflict punishments designed to humiliate or cause emotional distress, such as forcing prisoners to consume excrement or urine; shaving and painting their heads; and making them perform military-style exercises on command. In one case, reported in May 1993, a man and woman suspected of having illicit sexual relations were taken to the local police station, beaten and forced to re-enact the "crime", twice, on the floor of the interrogation room.[27]

Each year a large number of prisoners are reported to have died in custody as a result of ill-treatment or torture in police or prison custody. In the past five years, Amnesty International has recorded more than 100 suspicious deaths in custody of criminal suspects. However, the true figure may be much higher since the authorities usually cover up these deaths and opportunities for independent investigation are extremely limited.

CHAPTER 5

In January 1993 police in Indramayu, West Java, tortured a construction worker to death, hospitalized his wife and forced their nine-year-old son to watch, and to join in, his parents' torture, all in connection with a stolen wallet. Nine-year-old Junyonto was detained on suspicion of stealing the wallet on 16 January 1993. In the police station he was beaten on both feet and burned with cigarettes. The child then told the police he had stolen the wallet and given it to his parents.

The following day his mother, Dasmen, and his father, Sudarmono, were detained. Dasmen was beaten and kicked repeatedly by police but still denied any knowledge of the wallet. Her interrogators then tied her legs together, suspended her upside down from the ceiling, and tugged and pulled at her hair while continuing their questioning. Then the police brought in Junyonto and forced him to beat his mother. She lost consciousness, still denying any knowledge of the wallet, and was rushed to hospital where she remained in a coma for three days. Sudarmono was tortured the next day. Junyonto, who was made to watch, said that his father was repeatedly kicked and punched until he collapsed. He was rushed to hospital but was dead on arrival.

A local outcry forced the police to promise that those responsible would be brought to justice. Five police personnel were officially reported to have been detained and transferred to the Military Police for questioning. Nothing more was heard after these announcements. By mid-1994 it was not known whether any of the suspects had been charged.

Torture and ill-treatment is often employed to teach prisoners a lesson or to exact personal revenge. In November 1992 Antony Ginting, a bus conductor from Deli Tua, North Sumatra, was abducted, beaten, burned with cigarettes, and shot repeatedly in the legs by police officers who suspected him of stealing from their barracks. According to his own account, the police officers detained him without a warrant, tied his hands and forced him into a pick-up truck.

As they drove, the officers interrogated Antony Ginting, stopping several times to beat him, threaten him with their pistols, rub chillies in his eyes and burn him with cigarettes when he refused to confess. During one stop, three officers forced him to kneel and then urinated in his face. When they reached a cocoa plantation outside the town, Antony Ginting was ordered out of the truck and tied to a tree. During the interrogation that followed, one police

POWER AND IMPUNITY

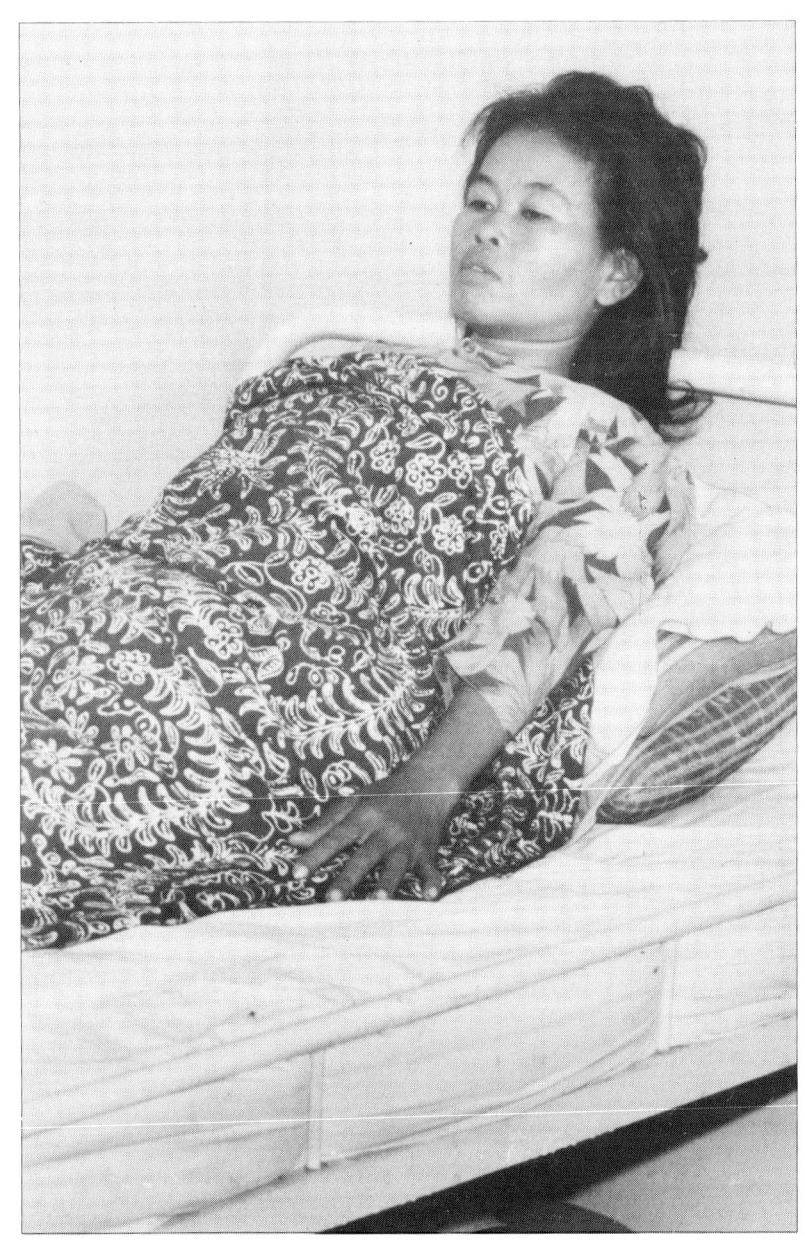

Dasmen recovering from torture inflicted by police in Indramayu, West Java, when her nine-year-old son was suspected of stealing a wallet. © *Tempo*

CHAPTER 5

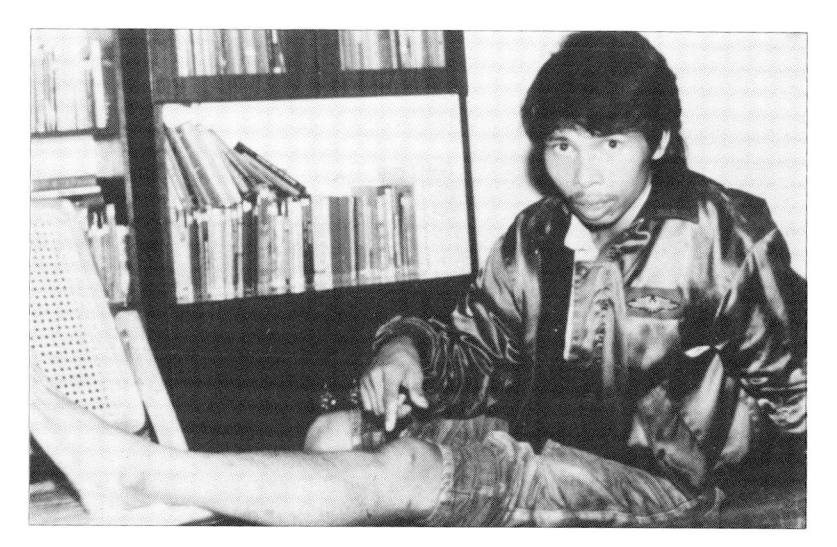

Antony Ginting, a bus conductor, was severely tortured by police officers in North Sumatra who suspected him of theft.© Yayasan Pijar

officer used a length of wood to beat him violently across the knees and other parts of his body. Another shot him 12 times in the legs. Others smashed his fingers with a hammer and stabbed his head with a screwdriver until blood flowed. Antony Ginting fell unconscious and awoke in hospital.

After two months in hospital recovering from his injuries, Antony Ginting was again detained by the police and charged with theft. Fearing further torture, he confessed and was later sentenced to five months in jail. After his release in August 1993, he filed formal complaints about his treatment. In November the Deli Tua police chief admitted to journalists that the police had ill-treated Antony Ginting, and said an internal inquiry had been conducted. He stated: "...if members of my unit are guilty, then my superiors will deal with them". However, by mid-1994, none of the seven police involved in the incident had been charged or punished.

Even when the suspected perpetrators of torture are charged and tried, they are often acquitted or receive very light sentences. In December 1992 Djatmiko, an inmate at Sragen Prison in Central Java, was beaten to death by prison guards. The authorities offered several conflicting accounts of the incident. The prison director claimed Djatmiko had died after falling and hitting his head. One prison official told Djatmiko's family that he had died of a stomach illness, and another said he had been hit by a car while running an errand for prison officials. The final explanation offered by prison and Ministry of Justice officials was that Djatmiko had died of injuries sustained in a fight with prison guards. However, police investigations indicated that as many as 12 prison officers may have been involved in the assault, while an autopsy revealed that Djatmiko had been repeatedly beaten about the head and that his neck had been broken.

Four prison guards were brought to trial in Sragen District Court in March 1993. During the trial the prosecution presented evidence that the accused had taken turns kicking, punching and beating Djatmiko, and that one of them had struck him repeatedly over the head with a folding metal chair until he collapsed and died. The defendants admitted these allegations but claimed that they had been acting in self-defence. They were charged with assault resulting in death, which carries a maximum penalty of 12 years. In November 1993, all four defendants were acquitted. On hearing the verdict, Djatmiko's father, a farm labourer, cried out: "It isn't fair! They have killed a man, how can they walk free?".

6
Political imprisonment and unfair trial

The New Order Government has made a habit of jailing its political opponents. An estimated 3,000 prisoners have been held on political charges since 1966, most of them convicted after unfair trials. Hundreds of thousands more have been detained without charge or trial for up to 14 years, and some have "disappeared" in custody.

Patterns of imprisonment

Some 350 political prisoners are currently held in jails throughout Indonesia and East Timor. Many of them neither used nor advocated violence and are prisoners of conscience. They include advocates of independence for East Timor, Aceh and Irian Jaya, as well as Islamic activists, former PKI members, university students, farmers, workers, and human rights activists. They are in prison for crimes such as possessing banned novels, criticizing the electoral system, peacefully resisting eviction, disseminating information about human rights violations, holding peaceful flag-raising ceremonies, advocating closer ties among Muslims, criticizing *Pancasila*, and organizing peaceful demonstrations.

Political trials in Indonesia and East Timor routinely fail to meet international standards of fairness. They are effectively show trials, characterized by the following general features:

- Once charges have been filed, guilt is assumed and conviction is a foregone conclusion.

- Defendants are routinely denied access to legal counsel of their choice, and defence lawyers are often refused access to court documents before the trial starts.

- Political cases are often handled by inexperienced, court-appointed lawyers who provide an inadequate defence.
- Defendants are often convicted on the basis of uncorroborated confessions or testimony extracted under duress.
- Trials are conducted in Indonesian, which is not always understood by defendants, and competent translators are not always provided.
- Defendants are frequently denied the right to cross-examine prosecution witnesses, while witnesses for the defence are often barred.
- Evidence of ill-treatment, torture and other irregularities in the pre-trial process are routinely ignored by the courts.
- Defence lawyers, prosecutors and judges are subjected to pressure from military and government authorities to ensure a guilty verdict.

The charges are often so vague, the evidence of guilt so patently thin, and the sentencing so draconian that political trials are clearly designed as a deterrent. They are also intended to foster the illusion that Indonesia is governed by the rule of law. Far from demonstrating a commitment to the rule of law, political trials demonstrate the arbitrariness of the judicial system, and how readily it can be influenced by those in power, particularly the military. This was neatly summarized by a military commander in Aceh who told lawyers from the Indonesian Legal Aid Institute in 1991: "You can eat your [Code of Criminal Procedure]. It doesn't apply here".

The treatment of political detainees generally improves after they have been sentenced and transferred to the prison system. Yet serious problems remain, particularly in more isolated areas and in high security prisons where access to lawyers, doctors and relatives may be heavily restricted. There are periodic reports of the injury or death in custody of political prisoners in such prisons. Correspondence to and from political prisoners is often censored or intercepted. Corruption is rife in the Indonesian prison system, and prisoners without access to an independent source of income or basic daily necessities face serious difficulties.

Some political prisoners benefit from the rules on remission of sentences. Remissions of up to four months are granted annually on national independence day to all prisoners considered to have behaved well. Recently revised regulations allow for the conditional release of most prisoners after they have served two-thirds of their sentence, but other rule changes make early release unlikely for some. For example, a 1987 presidential decree means prisoners serving life sentences can only gain remission through a presidential pardon, and rules out remission for any prisoner whose death sentence has already been commuted to life imprisonment.

Political prisoners are seldom released unconditionally. Some of the conditions imposed contravene international human rights standards upholding the rights to freedom of thought, expression and opinion. Prisoners are required to demonstrate that they have reformed politically. Most must undergo political "re-education" in prison, and are required to swear allegiance to the state and *Pancasila* before release. Former political prisoners also face serious restrictions after their release. Many, including those who were never tried, must report to military or police authorities on a regular basis for years. Restrictions on their rights to vote, to travel and to work are also common. Sometimes these are extended to apply to their relatives as well.

Many thousands or prisoners have been detained arbitrarily, some for 14 years, without charge or trial. Arbitrary and incommunicado detention is routinely practised to intimidate suspected opponents and to gather political intelligence during counter-insurgency operations. It is also used to prevent or break up strikes, peaceful gatherings, demonstrations and exhibitions. This practice has been widely criticized, forcing a recent shift in official tactics. Arbitrary detention now tends to be short-term; suspects are interrogated, often threatened or ill-treated, but released within the 24-hour legal limit. This allows the authorities to disrupt peaceful protests, and to intimidate suspected leaders, and still claim to be acting "in accordance with the law". Mass arbitrary detentions have also been justified in the interests of "national security".

Many of those held in arbitrary, unacknowledged military custody "disappear", making them vulnerable to torture and extrajudicial execution. This problem has been most acute in Aceh and East Timor, but conditions conducive to "disappearance" exist wherever the authorities are able to invoke the interests of "national security". In such situations the legal provisions designed to protect detainees' rights are either ignored or superseded by

POWER AND IMPUNITY

An East Timorese student is dragged to a police van during a demonstration in Jakarta on 19 November 1991 against the Santa Cruz massacre one week earlier. Dozens of demonstrators were arrested. © EPA *Photo*

CHAPTER 6

exceptional laws. The danger is greatest where detainees are held by units of the counter-insurgency force *Kopassus*. In the words of one Acehnese: "If you're taken away by the military you have a 50-50 chance of coming back. If you're taken by *Kopassus* you can forget it."

East Timor

Many thousands of East Timorese have been detained without charge or trial since the invasion of 1975, several hundreds of whom subsequently "disappeared". Hundreds of others have been convicted of opposing Indonesian rule in show trials that began in the mid-1980s. As the UN does not recognize Indonesia's sovereignty over East Timor, the competence of Indonesian courts to try East Timorese for opposition to Indonesian rule is open to question.

As of mid-1994 some 20 East Timorese were serving sentences ranging from a few years to life imprisonment for subversion, "expressing hostility" to the government or other political crimes. Most were accused of organizing the procession to the Santa Cruz cemetery in November 1991, or the peaceful protest against the massacre held in Jakarta later that month. Many were held incommunicado and tortured while being interrogated. The comments of prosecutors and judges during their trials indicated that they were being punished principally because they had contributed to the government's international embarrassment.

Among those tried in 1992 were Francisco Miranda Branco, who was sentenced to 15 years' imprisonment, and Gregorio da Cunha Saldanha, sentenced to life imprisonment. They were convicted of subversion for organizing the procession to the Santa Cruz cemetery. Gregorio da Cunha Saldanha said that he and other detainees had been "...obliged to give an explanation in accordance with the wishes of the investigators, not according to the true facts". Fernando Araujo and João Freitas da Camara were also convicted of subversion. They were sentenced to nine and 10 years' imprisonment for organizing the Jakarta protest march. In his verdict the judge said that Fernando Araujo was guilty of "undermining the Indonesia government and disgracing the nation in the eyes of the international community", because he had sent information about human rights violations to the ICRC and to Amnesty International.

The prime example of a political show trial in East Timor was that of Timorese resistance leader, Xanana Gusmão, who was

POWER AND IMPUNITY

East Timorese resistance leader, Xanana Gusmão, enters the courtroom in Dili, escorted by police officers. He was subjected to an unfair trial and sentenced to life imprisonment in May 1993 for rebellion and illegal possession of firearms. His sentence was later reduced to 20 years' imprisonment. © Reuters

CHAPTER 6

sentenced to life imprisonment for rebellion and illegal possession of firearms on 21 May 1993. Conscious of the strong international criticism of its human rights record in East Timor, the government took unusual steps to make Xanana Gusmão's trial appear open and fair. Selected foreign journalists, diplomats and some international human rights organizations were allowed to observe the trial. In an effort to further appease international opinion, in August 1993 the President reduced Xanana Gusmão's sentence to 20 years' imprisonment. However, long before the trial started it was clear that Xanana Gusmão was unlikely to get a fair hearing.

Xanana Gusmão was captured on 20 November 1992, and held in secret military custody for 17 days before ICRC representatives were permitted to see him. He was denied access to a lawyer while under interrogation, and was not allowed to appoint legal counsel of his choice, as required by law. Lawyers from the Indonesian Legal Aid Institute were not permitted to visit him, despite having been given power of attorney by his relatives. A defence lawyer was finally appointed on 26 January 1993, six days before the trial began.

The trial itself was marked by the violation of basic international and domestic standards of fairness. Prosecution witnesses, many of them political detainees, were subjected to undue pressure from military authorities. Fear of official reprisals meant that few witnesses would testify for the defence. Neither Xanana Gusmão nor many of the witnesses were fluent in Indonesian, the language of the proceedings; the translation provided was incomplete and inaccurate. Most importantly, the judge allowed Xanana Gusmão to read only two pages of his 29-page defence plea, claiming that it was "irrelevant".

In addition to those tried, at least 400 East Timorese have been held without charge or trial, for periods ranging from a few days to several months, since late 1991. Many were denied access to their relatives, lawyers and the ICRC; some were ill-treated and tortured. About 70 East Timorese were arrested after the November 1991 Jakarta protest; 46 were detained for two months without charge. As a condition of release, all were made to sign affidavits renouncing their peaceful political beliefs and stating their willingness to face legal sanctions should they commit "offences" in the future. Shortly before a visit by UN envoy Amos Wako in February 1992, security forces briefly detained scores of East Timorese youths and sent them on "guidance courses" for the duration of the visit. The capture of Xanana Gusmão sparked off a further wave of arrests. More than 70 people, including several of his relatives, were taken into custody. Most were held incommunicado and some were tortured. Further detentions preceded a visit to the territory by a delegation of US House of Representatives Foreign Affairs Committee staff in September 1993. The practice of short-term arbitrary detention continues.

Aceh

At least 50 people have been sentenced to prison terms of between three years and life since 1991 for their alleged links to *Aceh Merdeka*. All were convicted in unfair trials under the Anti-Subversion Law, and at least 24 appeared to be prisoners of conscience, having neither used nor advocated violence. Thousands of others were arbitrarily detained between 1989 and 1994, and many are feared to have "disappeared".

Trials of the alleged leadership of *Aceh Merdeka* — including university lecturers, civil servants and school teachers — began in March 1991. The public prosecutor acknowledged that members of this group "were not armed" but charged that they were "...the brains which planned the terrorist actions" of *Aceh Merdeka*. There was little or no evidence that any of this group had advocated violence or planned violent acts; in fact, some appeared to have argued openly against violence.

These trials were partly intended to answer international criticism of government human rights abuse in the territory, and to demonstrate that the government upholds the rule of law. Yet, at virtually every stage of the process, defendants in the *Aceh Merdeka* cases encountered treatment at odds with minimal guarantees in Indonesian and international law. Most were held incommunicado, without charge, for up to several months. Few, if any, were allowed visits from relatives until their trial had begun and many families were not officially notified of the reasons for the prisoners' arrests or their whereabouts.

More serious irregularities were evident in the investigation stage. The confessions of many defendants and the testimony of some prosecution witnesses were extracted under duress, and sometimes under torture. In June 1991 Amnesty International received a letter from a man who had been detained since late 1990 on suspicion of involvement with *Aceh Merdeka*. The letter

CHAPTER 6

described his arrest by the military, his treatment while in detention, and his trial:

> "The 15 days [after my arrest] witnessed the severest tortures inflicted on me during...interrogations by the military intelligence: beatings, cigarette burnings, whippings, electric shocks, water poured through the nose, forced drinking of urine, and curses....The interrogations were to force me to confess to things that I did not do, know of or see...so that they had the reasons to lock me up".

This man was sentenced to a lengthy prison term for subversion in 1991. Following an appeal to the High Court of Aceh, his sentence was increased. In his letter he asked that his name not be mentioned "...otherwise things will go worse at my end".

The use of torture to extract confessions from detainees in Aceh was facilitated by denying them other basic rights. None of the defendants were permitted to have a lawyer present during interrogation, or to consult one before their trials. Efforts by the Indonesian Legal Aid Institute to act on behalf of some defendants were obstructed by military and judicial authorities. Military authorities and the public prosecutor also threatened to return some detainees to military custody if they sought the assistance of a defence lawyer. The fear of further torture convinced most to cooperate.

Pre-trial irregularities were compounded at the trial stage. Judicial authorities ignored the testimony of witnesses and defendants that their confessions were extracted under torture. Fearing that the courts might not protect them from further abuse, some defendants decided not to testify about the torture they had suffered. A defendant convicted in 1991 explained why, in a letter to a friend:

> "A friend of mine...died in the prison on 13 December 1990, because of the torture; he vomited fresh blood when he was dying. Several others became completely paralysed. Ten or 11 were taken out during the night and killed outside the jail; their bodies have not been found....The threats being made against us at that time made me give in; a thing I deeply regret now."

Because defendants were not permitted lawyers of their choice, most were defended by court-appointed lawyers with little or no experience in political trials. As well as inexperience, lawyers faced almost insuperable obstacles in providing an effective defence for their clients. Most were appointed only a few days before the trial, and were unable to meet their clients until the first court session. They were denied access to crucial court documents, such as the interrogation depositions upon which the prosecution case was based.

The military authorities put heavy political pressure on defence lawyers. Before each trial, they were summoned for a briefing by military intelligence and warned not to mount too strong a defence. Most complied because to do otherwise could be construed as sympathy for *Aceh Merdeka* or because, out of fear, their clients had asked them to cooperate. Consequently, few defence lawyers attempted to challenge the charges against their clients and fewer still questioned procedural irregularities during arrest, detention and investigation. Prosecution witnesses were not rigorously cross-examined and witnesses were seldom called for the defence.

In addition to those jailed after unfair trials, at least 1,000 people were held in unacknowledged, incommunicado detention in Aceh and North Sumatra for periods ranging from a few days to more than a year between 1989 and 1994. Scores and possibly hundreds of Acehnese political detainees "disappeared" in custody, and many are feared to have been killed.

Arbitrary detention and "disappearance" in Aceh followed a definite pattern. Suspects were detained without warrant by military authorities. Relatives were not informed of the arrest or the place of detention. Those who made inquiries were routinely told that the person concerned was no longer in custody or had been transferred to another military camp or detention centre. The authorities did not keep public registers of detainees and made little effort to help the family locate them. Some relatives were interrogated or threatened. Requests for information made by national and international human rights organizations on behalf of families were generally ignored.

Some of those who "disappeared" reappeared later in custody. They included some 1,000 uncharged and untried political detainees who were conditionally released between September 1990 and March 1994. The official explanation for their release was that they had been found to have only a limited connection with *Aceh Merdeka*, and that they should be given an opportunity to reform politically. The releases were accompanied by official ceremonies intended to demonstrate the military's goodwill and respect for the rule of law. At a release ceremony in June 1991 the Regional Military Commander told political detainees: "Bear in mind that you are found guilty. But the level of your guilt is low, so we give you a chance to improve yourselves."[28]

Far from demonstrating a commitment to the rule of law, the releases highlighted the arbitrary nature of the original detentions. All the detainees had been denied the legal safeguards provided by Indonesia's Code of Criminal Procedure, none had been charged or tried but were presumed and treated as guilty, and some had been held incommunicado for more than a year.

Irian Jaya

More than 140 people have been jailed for subversion since 1989 for advocating Irian Jaya's independence. At least 50 remained in jail in mid-1994, over half of whom were prisoners of conscience, serving sentences of up to 20 years' imprisonment. Many of these prisoners are held in East Java, more than 1,500 miles away, making it difficult for their relatives to visit them.

Among those jailed in 1989 were Dr Thomas Wainggai and his wife, Teruko Wainggai, a Japanese national. They were convicted of subversion in September 1989 and sentenced to life and eight years' imprisonment respectively. Dr Wainggai was the leader of a group of 37 people who staged a peaceful flag-raising ceremony in December 1988 to proclaim the independent state of "West Melanesia". None of the group had used or advocated violence, a fact acknowledged by the Regional Military Commander for Irian Jaya one month before Dr Wainggai was sentenced:

> "*[It is] really nothing more than a diplomatic group....It is not an armed movement....He had got together a few people to act as functionaries of a new state but he hadn't got around to making any laws.*"

Teruko Wainggai and two other women, both sentenced to four years' imprisonment, were accused of sewing the flag used in the ceremony. Two women who led the opening and closing prayers received prison terms of four and five years, while a man who led the singing of "My Country Melanesia" was sentenced to six years. Fourteen participants who assisted in raising the flag were jailed for between four and eight years. More than 40 other suspected supporters of independence were arrested and tried for subversion in 1989 and 1990, and sentenced to up to 17 years' imprisonment. Most were accused of planning to commemorate the 1988 proclamation.

Available information about the trial of Dr Wainggai suggests that political trials in Irian Jaya have the same deficiencies noted elsewhere in Indonesia and in East Timor. Like most defendants in political trials, Dr Wainggai was presumed guilty. In August 1989, before the District Court had reached a verdict, the Regional Military Commander made a public statement clearly implying Dr Wainggai's guilt:

> "He got frustrated and carried out these activities like proclaiming a new country. That's subversion and has to be firmly put down according to the process of law."

Defence lawyers from the Legal Aid Institute were prevented from bringing a full complement of witnesses and had little time to cross-examine prosecution witnesses because of the schedule imposed by the court. In some of the trials, including that of Teruko Wainggai, the court proceedings were conducted in a language which the defendant did not understand well.

The defence lawyers themselves were threatened and intimidated. During the trial a military intelligence officer confiscated the cassette tape recorder used by the defence team to record the court's proceedings. Defence lawyers objected on the grounds that its use had not been forbidden by the court. However, the judge defended the military action, arguing that "...if it is a matter of security, then the security forces must be given complete authority", and warned the defence team against any further "funny business". When they lodged an official protest, the judge threatened them with contempt of court, and challenged the legality of their branch of the Legal Aid Institute.

Muslim activists

Hundreds of Muslims have been jailed in Indonesia over the past 15 years. Some were found guilty of acts of violence but scores were jailed solely for their peaceful beliefs and activities. Most were accused of criticizing the government, of undermining *Pancasila*, or of attempting to establish an Islamic state. As of mid-1994, an estimated 200 Muslim prisoners remained in jail, including at least 40 prisoners of conscience.

CHAPTER 6

Typical of many was Abdul Fatah Wiranagapati, a 69-year-old Muslim, sentenced to eight years' imprisonment in June 1992 for "undermining the state ideology" and attempting to establish an Islamic state. The court found that he had not used violence but had spread his ideas by holding meetings and preaching about Islamic law. In his verdict, the presiding judge said that Abdul Fatah Wiranagapati had "...used his preaching in mosques to disseminate anti-government propaganda".

The trials of Muslim activists have been uniformly unfair. Guilt appears to have been predetermined and evidence of innocence presented to the court has almost always been ignored. Only one of hundreds of defendants tried for subversion in the past 15 years is known to have been acquitted.

There is substantial evidence that the government, through its military intelligence agencies, has encouraged some Islamic groups to use violence. The purpose appears to have been to provide a pretext for widespread crack-downs against Muslim activists and to undermine lawful Muslim organizations, such as the PPP, the lawful Islamic party. Hundreds of people have been jailed since the late 1970s on the pretext that they were involved with these militant organizations. The detainees have included preachers, pamphleteers, Mosque officials and scholars.

One of the most significant series of Muslim trials began in 1985, a year after soldiers had massacred scores of protesters in Tanjung Priok, Jakarta. Once again there was evidence of military provocation, and again the violence was used to justify widespread arrests and prosecutions. Around half of the 200 people arrested in connection with the protest were subsequently brought to trial. Some were accused of acts of violence, but scores were sentenced to years in jail because of their peaceful beliefs. Several prominent opposition figures, including three members of the "Petition of Fifty" group, were also jailed after criticizing the government's handling of the affair and calling for an independent inquiry.

The next major series of trials began in 1986 and continued until 1989. The defendants were members of small Islamic communities, known as *usroh* and based in Central Java, which aimed to spread Islamic teachings and values. At least 40 *usroh* members were convicted of subversion, for allegedly seeking to establish an Islamic state and undermine *Pancasila*. Little or no evidence was presented to substantiate these allegations.

In early 1989 the spotlight shifted from the *usroh* groups after government troops attacked an alleged militant Islamic sect in Lampung, known by the name of its leader, Warsidi. In the aftermath of the assault, which may have left as many as 100 people dead, the government began a widespread crack-down against Muslims believed to be linked with the "Warsidi Gang". Scores of Muslim activists were arrested in subsequent months in Lampung, Nusa Tenggara Barat, West Java and 'Jakarta. Most were tried for subversion in 1989 and 1990. All were found guilty and sentenced to terms of up to life imprisonment.

PKI prisoners

A minute fraction of the more than 500,000 people arrested after the 1965 coup, about 1,000 in all, were brought to trial and sentenced to lengthy prison terms or condemned to death. At least 25 of those remained in prison in mid-1994, more than a quarter of a century after their arrest. Most were believed to be prisoners of conscience. In addition to those tried, hundreds of thousands were held without charge or trial for periods ranging from a few weeks to 14 years. In addition to those still in jail, a large number of former PKI prisoners remain under house arrest and face serious restrictions on their civil and political rights and freedom of movement.

Because of their advanced age, a number of PKI prisoners have died in custody; others suffer serious illnesses. Pudjo Prasetio, aged 68, was diagnosed in 1993 as suffering from Parkinson's Disease. A former shipbuilder and trade unionist, Pudjo Prasetio joined the PKI in the mid-1950s. He was arrested in 1967 in Central Java and held for 12 years before being tried and sentenced to life imprisonment for subversion. Because it was his only hope for release under the new law on remissions, Pudjo Prasetio requested presidential clemency but in March 1991 he learned that it had been denied. In a letter to a friend he wrote: "By the way, my request for clemency was refused by the president. It means that there's no more way to be released. If there's no political changes I'll be jailed forever." In mid-1994 Pudjo Prasetio remained in prison in Bali. Although he has received medical treatment, his health has continued to deteriorate.

A number of elderly PKI prisoners held in Cipinang prison are suffering from serious physical and mental disabilities. Ruslan Wijayasastra, aged 75, is almost totally paralysed and requires the constant assistance of fellow prisoners to walk and to carry out

CHAPTER 6

normal functions like rising from his bed and eating. Arrested in July 1968 and sentenced to death six years later, Ruslan was a member of the Central Committee of the PKI and an official of the PKI-affiliated peasant union. In March 1994 fellow political prisoners and human rights organizations appealed to the National Human Rights Commission for the release of Ruslan and others on humanitarian grounds, but the commission said that it was up to the President to grant clemency to those under sentence of death.

The trials of those accused of PKI membership or participation in the coup were uniformly unfair. The virulent anti-communism which followed the 1965 coup meant that few witnesses dared testify on behalf of suspected PKI members on trial for subversion. Defence lawyers acting for PKI members were accused of communist sympathies, threatened and harassed. Many of the witnesses were also prisoners, and in some cases the "evidence" they gave had been extracted under torture. There were also serious doubts about the impartiality of the judges, particularly those who headed the special

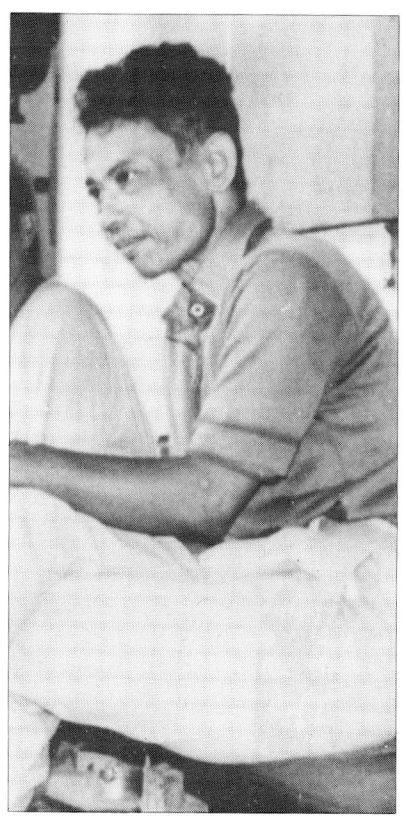

Pudjo Prasetio has been in prison since 1967 and is serving a life sentence for subversion. He is suffering from Parkinson's Disease. In May 1991 his request for clemency was refused. In a letter to a friend, he wrote: "It means that there's no more way to be released. If there's no political changes I'll be jailed forever."

military courts which sentenced high-ranking PKI members to long prison terms or death. Many PKI prisoners were denied the right to appeal; those allowed to appeal often waited 10 or 20 years to learn that their appeals had been rejected.

Years after their release, more than one million of those imprisoned as PKI members or supporters still face severe restrictions on their civil and political rights. Although most were never tried or found guilty of any offence, their identity cards are marked "ET", an acronym signifying "Former Political Prisoner". This mark carries with it a powerful political and social stigma, as well as real legal limitations, that affect not only former detainees but also their relatives, including many who were not even born at the time of the 1965 coup.

Former prisoners or PKI members, and often members of their families, are prohibited from working in any occupation which might give them the opportunity to influence public opinion, such as journalist, teacher, village head, actor, puppeteer or religious preacher. Severe restrictions on freedom of movement mean that they are effectively under house or town arrest, and must seek special permission to travel or even to move house.

Former PKI prisoners also suffer political restrictions. They are granted the right to vote only with the explicit approval of government and military authorities, after investigations to establish their political attitudes and behaviour. Before the June 1992 national elections, the government announced that 36,345 former PKI prisoners would not be permitted to vote. Political party candidates are required to undergo political screening before their nomination can be accepted; those who pass the test but are later discovered to have had some link to the PKI are likely to be forced from office.

Students

Dozens of students have been sentenced to prison terms ranging from a few months to nine years for their non-violent political activities. Many others have been detained without charge for short periods, apparently to disrupt their activities, however lawful, and to obtain information about their organizations.

Several university students and other young people have been sentenced to lengthy prison terms for possessing banned literary works. Bambang Subono was arrested on 9 June 1988 while selling copies of the novel "*Rumah Kaca*" ("Glass House") and other works

CHAPTER 6

Demonstrators gather outside the trial of Bambang Isti Nugroho in April 1989. Bambang was one of several students and young people arrested for possessing banned literary works. He was sentenced to eight years' imprisonment.

Pramoedya Ananta Toer, Indonesia's leading novelist, was imprisoned for 14 years after the 1965 coup. Since his release his movements have been restricted; all his books are banned. Students have been sentenced to long prison terms solely for possessing his works. © Reuters

POWER AND IMPUNITY

Student Bonar Tigor Naipospos was sentenced to eight-and-a-half years' imprisonment for possessing and distributing literature said to contain "communist" ideas. He was conditionally released in May 1994.

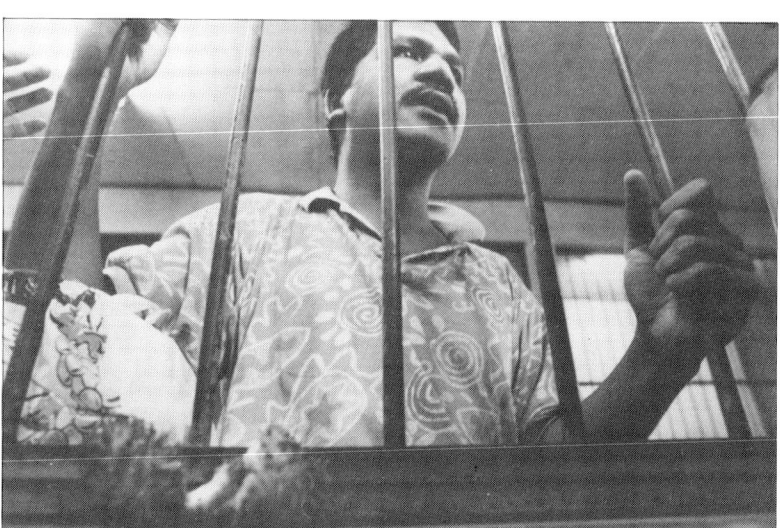

Nuku Soleiman, a human rights activist jailed for five years for "insulting" the President; he had demanded that President Suharto accept responsibility for past human rights violations. © *Yayasan Pijar*

CHAPTER 6

by the renowned Indonesian author, Pramoedya Ananta Toer. Bambang Isti Nugroho, a student at Gajah Mada University, Yogyakarta, was arrested in June 1988 on similar charges. The two were found guilty of subversion and sentenced to seven and eight years' imprisonment respectively. Another student, Bonar Tigor Naipospos, was arrested in Jakarta in June 1989, convicted of subversion and sentenced to eight-and-a-half years' imprisonment for possessing and distributing literature said to contain communist ideas, and for disseminating Marxist teachings in discussion groups and through his own writings. He was conditionally released in May 1994.

Students have also been jailed for their peaceful political and human rights activities. Nuku Soleiman was arrested on 25 November 1993 during a peaceful protest outside Indonesia's national parliament in Jakarta. He was accused of distributing stickers in which the acronym for the country's state-backed lottery (SDSB) was given a new meaning. The stickers read *Suharto Dalang Segala Bencana* — Suharto is the mastermind of all disasters — and cited numerous instances of serious human rights violations committed by Indonesian security forces since 1965.

Nuku Soleiman was sentenced to four years' imprisonment by the District Court of Central Jakarta on 24 February 1994, following a month-long show trial. He was charged with "insulting the President". In May 1994, following his appeal to the High Court, his sentence was increased to five years.

In his first defence statement, Nuku Soleiman described the atmosphere of the trial:

"Just look around! From the first day of the session, it is as if the army and police are in command here...In front of this building they have lined up trucks full of armed troops. At the entrance to this hall, they block my friends, my relatives, and the general public who want to attend this trial. In this court-room they have assigned plainclothes officers to occupy a large number of the chairs for visitors. As the trial began, a group of police officers equipped with rattan clubs and canes marched in here, though there was not the slightest sign of unrest in this hall...I feel this as terror, as intimidation. Does the Council of Judges not also feel the same?... Is it not the case that such an atmosphere is bound to influence the verdict of the Court?"

POWER AND IMPUNITY

Yeni Damayanti (top, centre) was one of 21 students who were sentenced to six months' imprisonment for "insulting" the President in May 1994. The students were arrested during a peaceful demonstration in Jakarta in December 1993 calling on President Suharto to accept responsibility for past human rights violations.

Shortly after Nuku Soleiman's sentencing, the District Attorney's office in Jakarta announced that 21 students were to be brought to trial on similar charges. They were arrested in Jakarta on 14 December 1993, during a peaceful demonstration calling on parliament to hold a special session to investigate the President's responsibility for past human rights abuses. In May 1994 they were sentenced to six months' imprisonment for "insulting the President".

Farmers and land activists

Members of farming communities involved in land disputes with private or official bodies, and activists working with them, have suffered a range of abuses, including intimidation, death threats, attempted murder and imprisonment. Some are prisoners of conscience.

CHAPTER 6

Some 300 farmers from the villages of Cijayanti and Rancamaya in West Java, and several human rights activists, were detained by military authorities after a peaceful demonstration outside the office of a government minister in Jakarta on 24 September 1993. They were protesting against being evicted by real estate development companies. The protest followed more than a year of intimidation and one case of attempted murder by company officials against the farmers. Although most were released without charge after questioning, some were ill-treated and threatened with death, and at least two were re-arrested. They were prisoners of conscience.

Among those held for questioning was M.H. Sinaga, Director of the Ampera Legal Aid Institute (LBH-Ampera). He alleged that he was ill-treated and threatened with a pistol during his interrogation.

Ahmad Jauhari, a staff member of the same organization, received written death threats and had his house wrecked less than two weeks after the demonstration. The attackers' identity was unknown, but the timing and

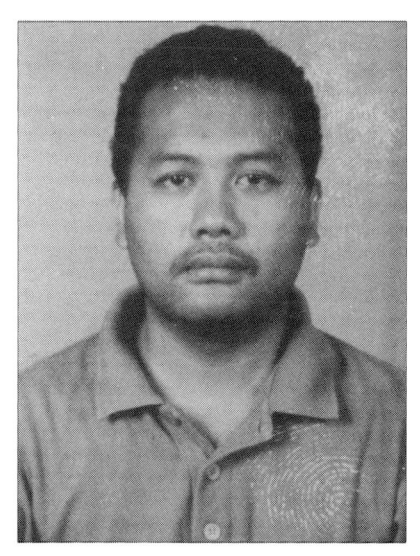

Human rights activist Dedi Ekadibrata was imprisoned in 1994 because of his non-violent activities on behalf of the farming communities in Cijayanti, West Java, who were threatened with eviction from their land. © Dok Forum

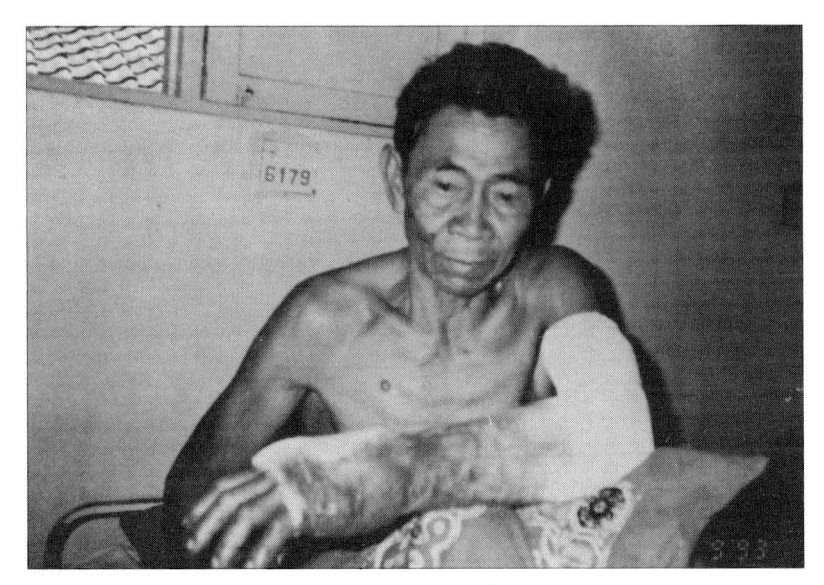

Haji Dodo, a 70-year-old farmer from Cijayanti, who was almost killed by private security guards trying to evict him from his land in early 1994.
© *Yayasan Pijar*

context of the attack raised suspicions of police involvement or complicity.

Two others were later imprisoned in connection with the case. On 11 October, a farmer from Rancamaya, Cheppy Sudrajat, was sentenced to 10 months' imprisonment for his role in organizing the September 1993 protest. In early 1994, Dedi Ekadibrata, another human rights activist connected with LBH-Ampera, was tried and sentenced to 18 months in prison. He was arrested on 9 November 1993 and charged with inciting a January 1993 attack on the base camp of the real estate company in Cijayanti. However, human rights lawyers believed that he was arrested because of his non-violent activities on behalf of the farming communities in the area.

Workers and trade unionists

The government has used various methods, including short-term detention and imprisonment, to silence the advocates of workers' rights, and to undermine independent unions such as the Indonesian Workers' Welfare Union (SBSI).

CHAPTER 6

At least 19 SBSI members including the national chairman, Muchtar Pakpahan, a member of its national executive council, Sunarty, and the chairman of its Central Java executive council, Trisjanto, were detained on 10 February 1994, on the eve of a national strike. They were apparently arrested to prevent them from organizing the strike, and to intimidate workers from supporting it. All 19 were released within a few days, but Muchtar Pakpahan, Sunarty and Trisjanto were charged with incitement and expressing hostility towards the government.

More than 100 workers and activists were detained during a wave of labour unrest in Medan which degenerated into an anti-Chinese riot in mid-April 1994. As of early May 1994, at least 50 remained in police custody. Most were charged with criminal offences, such as destruction of property and assault but at least five officials of SBSI-Medan were held for their role in organizing the demonstrations. They were apparently detained solely for their non-violent labour activism. The military has alleged that the SBSI was responsible for the anti-Chinese violence and had links with the PKI, allegations which could be used as to justify bringing its leaders to trial for subversion or other political crimes.

One of the five SBSI-Medan officials detained was the branch secretary, Riswan Lubis. He was arrested on 15 April 1994. Colleagues who saw him in detention at Medan police headquarters several days later said he had apparently been beaten. Another was Amosi Telaumbanua, chairman of SBSI-Medan, arrested on 29 April. A long-time labour activist, Amosi Telaumbanua had been arrested by the military on at least three previous occasions and twice ill-treated or tortured while in custody. Indonesian human rights lawyers feared that these and other SBSI officials could be charged with incitement, and possibly with subversion. If found guilty of incitement, they would face a maximum term of seven years in prison; if convicted of subversion, a maximum penalty of death.

7

The death penalty

The death penalty can be imposed for a wide range of crimes in Indonesia. Its use has increased steadily over the past two decades. Between 1985 and 1994 there were at least 30 executions, compared to four in the previous decade. Although most of those sentenced to death had been convicted of murder, most of those executed were political prisoners convicted of subversion. Of the 30 people known to have been executed since 1985, 27 were political prisoners. Most were condemned to death in show trials; some had been awaiting execution for almost a quarter of a century. Those still on death row in mid-1994 included six elderly men sentenced in the late 1960s and early 1970s for involvement in the 1965 coup or for membership of the PKI, and dozens of convicted criminal prisoners.

Some government and judicial authorities appear sensitive to arguments against the death penalty. In a surprising decision taken in 1988, the Indonesian Supreme Court ruled that the death penalty was inconsistent with *Pancasila*. Nevertheless, the government has defended retaining the death penalty on the grounds that it serves as a deterrent to serious crime. However, since most victims of execution have been political prisoners, it would appear that the death penalty has been used principally to assert the government's political power and to deter potential political opponents.

The government has also been at pains to demonstrate that, in carrying out executions, it has acted in accordance with the law and within its right as a sovereign state. International protests are rejected as external interference in Indonesia's affairs. When it was rumoured that seven PKI prisoners were scheduled for execution in March 1990, the Armed Forces Commander told journalists:

CHAPTER 7

"The issue of executions is an internal matter of Indonesia, an affair concerning our national interests, our sovereignty and our freedom. Therefore outsiders should not interfere in our affairs. Write that in big letters."

The government's preoccupation with the formal legality of the death penalty, and its attacks on foreign interference on the issue, have diverted attention from fundamental questions about how the death penalty constitutes, or contributes to, serious human rights violations.

Killing the innocent

In any judicial system that allows the death penalty there is always the risk that an innocent person may be executed. In a judicial system characterized by corruption and lack of independence, as is Indonesia's, the possibility of wrongful execution is increased.

Dozens of the PKI political prisoners already executed and others still awaiting execution were condemned after unfair trials in special military courts, in which there was no right of appeal. Prisoners sentenced to death by the civilian courts do have a right to appeal, although the appeals process is seriously flawed.

The final legal remedy available to prisoners under sentence of death in Indonesia is presidential clemency. Since an execution may not be carried out until a request for clemency has been rejected, the denial of clemency removes the last formal barrier to execution. Clemency is seldom granted, and executions often follow swiftly after it has been denied. Prisoners therefore fear that to request clemency is simply to hasten their execution and some therefore refuse to request it.

A prisoner's refusal to ask for clemency causes the authorities certain legal and administrative problems. Judicial and executive authorities have sometimes requested clemency for prisoners either without their knowledge or against their will. This suggests that the request for clemency is little more than a legal formality subject to arbitrary use by both the judicial and the executive branches of the government.

Cruel treatment

The experience of spending many years awaiting execution is itself a form of torture or cruel and inhuman treatment. This is the norm in Indonesia; many prisoners sentenced to death have spent more than two decades on death row.

The government has explained such delays as evidence of its respect for the rule of law. In 1990 the government told the UN Commission on Human Rights that a 24-year delay in executing four political prisoners was the inevitable result of a fair and rigorous judicial process:

> "...the process of applying for clemency in their own cases, took a considerable amount of time and is, in fact, an indication that the defendants were afforded every legal remedy, including that of appeal to the higher courts."[29]

This explanation was misleading. It deliberately obscured the element of political calculation which motivated the timing of the executions. It also attempted to deflect attention from the clear evidence of official indifference to the suffering of the prisoners and their families. These four prisoners had waited up to 18 years to learn that their appeals to a higher court had been denied and a further three years to learn that their requests for presidential clemency, submitted in 1987, had been rejected.

Many of the procedures surrounding the implementation of the death penalty — including the decision to execute a prisoner — are shrouded in official secrecy. Those on death row often do not know they are about to die until one day they are led from their cells for pre-execution processing. From that moment they have 74 hours to live. Their relatives and friends often find out after it is too late, compounding their suffering. The immediate families of two of the four prisoners executed in February 1990 learned of their deaths from friends who had heard the news on the radio.

Indonesian lawyers have argued that the long delays on death row constitute an infringement of the Criminal Code, which stipulates that a prisoner may not be punished twice for the same crime. The Legal Aid Institute (LBH) believes that prisoners who have remained in jail for more than 20 years have already served one sentence, making their execution illegal.

Political prisoners

Of the 30 prisoners executed since 1985, 22 were sentenced to death for their alleged involvement in the 1965 coup or for membership

CHAPTER 7

of the PKI. Five others were Muslim political prisoners convicted of subversion and other crimes.

Between late 1989 and early 1990 six PKI prisoners were executed. This gave rise to serious concern for the remaining PKI prisoners on death row — Ruslan Wijayasastra, Iskandar Subekti (who died in 1993), Asep Suryaman, Bungkus, Marsudi, Isnanto and Sukatno. Concern was heightened by rumours that they were scheduled for execution on 11 March 1990. In the event the executions were not carried out, but the government stated that it would not bow to pressure from foreign governments or Amnesty International not to carry them out in future. All remain in imminent danger of execution.

Recent statements and actions by Indonesian government authorities have given rise to particular concern for the safety of Sukatno, a former member of parliament and PKI member who has been in prison for more than 25 years. On 4 September 1993 President Suharto wrote to the Secretary General of the Inter-Parliamentary Union (IPU) stating that there were no grounds for granting a stay of execution, as urged by the IPU:

"*In compliance with your request, I have instructed the Minister of Justice and other related agencies to make a review of and recommendations on the case. The result of the review revealed that the convicted person has never asked for clemency nor has shown any sign of remorse over his criminal actions, which have claimed many lives and created serious unrest in our community....Consequently, there is no choice for the Indonesian Government but to duly implement the execution of the court's verdict.*"[30]

Sukatno was sentenced to death in 1971 for his alleged involvement in the 1965 coup and his membership of the PKI. The High Court rejected his appeal in 1975, and the Supreme Court upheld this ruling in 1985. Sukatno has consistently refused to request clemency, because he maintains that he is innocent and because he apparently fears that this would remove the final legal obstacle to his execution. However, he has been pressured by prison and military authorities to request clemency or to state in writing that he does not wish to do so. These actions, and the long and uncertain stay in prison he has already endured, have exacerbated the inherent cruelty of his sentence.

The pressure exerted on Sukatno coincided with expressions

POWER AND IMPUNITY

Sukatno was sentenced to death in 1971 in an unfair trail and is in imminent danger of execution. A former member of parliament, he has been imprisoned continuously since his arrest in July 1968.

of concern on his behalf by the IPU. In February 1991, the Indonesian delegation to the IPU revealed that because Sukatno had consistently refused to ask for clemency, a request would be submitted on his behalf. It was later revealed that the District Court of Central Jakarta had requested clemency in 1986, without Sukatno's knowledge. Commenting on the procedures by which the petition for clemency had been submitted, a resolution of the Inter-Parliamentary Council stated that:

"...the appeal on his behalf and against his will, lodged by the court that tried him, constitutes an arbitrary measure [so that]...Mr Sukatno's execution would be arbitrary and unlawful and constitute a gross violation of human rights."[31]

Nevertheless, President Suharto formally rejected the clemency appeal on 13 May 1992, thereby removing the last legal obstacle to Sukatno's execution.

Criminal suspects

The death sentence has also been imposed for murder and drugs-related offences in recent years. At least four death

CHAPTER 7

sentences have been imposed for drug-trafficking since 1985, although no one had been executed for the offence by mid-1994. Over the same period at least 12 people have been sentenced to death for murder, and three are known to have been executed, although the numbers may be higher.

As in most countries that retain the death penalty for drug offences, the rationale for its use in Indonesia is that it will deter drug traffickers more effectively than other punishments. However, despite hundreds of executions around the world during the past five years, there is no compelling evidence of a decline in drug-trafficking which could be attributed to the use of the death penalty. It is usually the weakest links in a drug smuggling chain who are caught and executed, while the syndicate's leaders walk free.

Kamjai Khong Thavorn, a Thai seaman, was sentenced to death for drug smuggling by an Indonesian court in 1988. Despite considerable doubt about his guilt, evidence that his trial was unfair and humanitarian concern for his impoverished family in Bangkok, all of his appeals, including a request for presidential clemency, have been rejected.

Kamjai Khong Thavorn was arrested in August 1987 in Samarinda, East Kalimantan, after Indonesian customs officials conducting a routine inspection of his ship discovered 17.76 kilograms of heroin in his cabin. Evidence which emerged after his trial suggested strongly that Kamjai Khong Thavorn was either innocent or else a very minor actor in a large drugs smuggling operation. According to defence lawyers, two men questioned by Thai police in June 1991 admitted that they had placed a bag containing 20 packages of "horse medicine" (heroin) in Kamjai's Khong Thavorn's cabin, on instructions from a Japanese national.

Serious doubts have been raised about the fairness of the trial. The original trial, as well as all subsequent appeals and legal procedures, were conducted in Indonesian, which Kamjai Khong Thavorn could not speak or understand at the time. There have also been suggestions that some of the prosecution evidence may have been falsified.

Some stages of the appeals process appear to have been carried out without the knowledge or agreement of either the defendant or his lawyers. Kamjai Khong Thavorn's lawyers were not informed of the appeal to the Supreme Court or of the application for presidential clemency. The lawyers have argued that the clemency appeal was legally invalid because it was submitted by prison

POWER AND IMPUNITY

Kamjai Khong Thavorn, a Thai seaman, was sentenced to death for drug smuggling in January 1988. Despite considerable doubt about his guilt and evidence that his trial was unfair, all his appeals have been rejected. He is in imminent danger of execution.© Tempo

officials without Kamjai's full agreement or understanding. The appeal included an admission of guilt and was later used by government and judicial authorities as evidence against him, and as a reason for upholding the death sentence.

Kamjai Khong Thavorn was the sole breadwinner for his wife and two children and an extended family which still lives in a poor neighbourhood in Bangkok. His family only learned of his imminent execution in 1991 through media reports in Thailand.

Citing irregularities in the trial process, evidence of his innocence and humanitarian concern for his family, in May 1991 Kamjai Khong Thavorn's lawyers requested the Supreme Court to review the case. The Supreme Court refused the request in September 1992 on the grounds that there was no new evidence to be heard, and that clemency had already been denied. In early January 1993 lawyers submitted a second request for presidential clemency. The President's decision had not been announced by mid-1994.

8

Government human rights initiatives

The government has recently taken a number of widely publicized human rights initiatives. A National Human Rights Commission was established by Presidential Decree in June 1993 and its 25 members were appointed in December. A group of international journalists was invited to visit East Timor in February 1994, and in April the government announced publicly that it wished to discuss human rights with Amnesty International. Seminars and workshops on human rights have become more frequent and the national media is increasingly able and willing to report and comment on such matters.

To the extent that these steps constitute a genuine shift in official attitudes, they represent an important step forward. Unfortunately, they have yet to be matched by concrete legal and procedural measures to remedy past abuses, or to prevent future human rights violations. The government has continued to impede independent human rights monitoring by limiting access to East Timor and Indonesia, and by restricting the activities of domestic and international human rights organizations, including Amnesty International and the ICRC. And while preventing others from doing so, the government itself has failed to conduct thorough, independent investigations of serious human rights violations or to ensure that the suspected perpetrators are brought to justice.

Shaping the human rights debate

Stung by domestic and international criticism of its human rights record, the government has recently tried to recast the debate about human rights. Its position constitutes a frontal assault on two fundamental principles: first, that human rights are universal rights which apply to all people regardless of where they live; and second, that the international community has both a right and a duty to help prevent human rights violations wherever they occur.

For the sake of its image abroad, the government stresses that it recognizes the universality of UN human rights standards but argues that, in implementing these standards, states must be free to act according to their particular cultural, historical and political circumstances. In practice, such freedom amounts to a licence for state violation of basic civil and political rights.

The government's central premise is that the principles enshrined in international human rights covenants are not universal, but reflect liberal "western" values which emphasize civil and political rights at the expense of economic, social and cultural rights. What is required, in the official view, is greater emphasis on the rights of the community, the "nation" and the state. More specifically, the government stresses that concern for human rights must not be allowed to interfere with a nation's "right to develop" or to infringe on its national sovereignty.

The government contends that Indonesia should be guided by its own "indigenous" conception of human rights, as embodied in the 1945 Constitution and *Pancasila*. These provide only the sketchiest outline of basic rights, and do not impose any serious constraints on the authority or behaviour of the state.

The government has also attempted to deflect attention from its own human rights record by accusing others of exploiting the issue for political and economic ends. Not without some justification, it has accused "the West" of hypocrisy, noting that the governments which criticize Indonesia are themselves often guilty of human rights abuse. It has taken a strong position against the linking of human rights to aid and trade relations, accusing western governments of using human rights to disguise selfish economic and political aims. Posturing of this kind has helped to popularize the Indonesian Government's discourse about human rights, but it has done little to protect the rights of ordinary people.

The government has also sought to legitimize its own concept of human rights in international fora. As Chairman of the Non-Aligned Movement (NAM), Indonesia played a critical role in framing the September 1992 "Jakarta Message", which enshrined the principles of non-interference and national sovereignty in the implementation of human rights principles. As host and chair of the UN's Second Asia Pacific Workshop on Human Rights held in

Jakarta in January 1993, the government was able to build strong regional support for these principles.

The Indonesian Government has also argued strongly against any enhancement of the power of international human rights institutions that it does not dominate. During the UN World Conference on Human Rights in Vienna in June 1993, for example, it unsuccessfully opposed the creation of a UN Special Commissioner for Human Rights to coordinate, and give additional political weight to, the UN's various human rights bodies.

The government argues that international human rights protection can only be accomplished through "cooperation", not through outside monitoring. This appeal for a "cooperative" approach appears designed to evade the external scrutiny of the government's human rights record which international law requires. It is clear that government and military officials continue to view actual scrutiny as unwarranted interference in Indonesia's internal affairs. Foreign governments and international organizations which criticize Indonesia's human rights record are accused of being "anti-Indonesian" or guilty of cultural arrogance.

The government has also sought to vilify the proponents of universal human rights at home. Military and other state officials have repeatedly warned that "communists" and other "extremists" are using human rights issues for "subversive ends".

Liberalism and "western-style human rights" are portrayed as foreign ideologies inconsistent with Indonesian values: those who espouse them are accused of treachery or subversion. Yet the students, farmers, lawyers, workers, academics and others who have been outspoken in defence of universal human rights, are no less Indonesian than the government which pretends to speak on behalf of Indonesian "culture" and "values".

Cooperation with UN human rights bodies

Indonesia became a member of the UN Commission on Human Rights in 1991. As such, it bears a special responsibility to implement the recommendations enumerated in that body's statements and resolutions. Yet, with some minor exceptions, it has not done so and has indicated that it does not feel bound to abide by the provisions of certain resolutions. Its record of cooperation with the UN's thematic human rights mechanisms has been similarly chequered.

The government invited the UN's Special Rapporteur on torture

CHAPTER 8

to visit Indonesia and East Timor in late 1991. His report concluded that torture is commonplace in Indonesia and East Timor, and offered 11 concrete recommendations for its prevention, including the following: the government should accede to major human rights covenants; detainees' right of access to a lawyer should be rigorously upheld; illegally obtained evidence should not be admissible in court; the Anti-Subversion Law should be repealed; officials found guilty of committing or condoning torture should be punished; the civilian courts should have jurisdiction over human rights offences committed by members of the armed forces; and a national commission on human rights, with independent investigative powers, should be established.

As of mid-1994, more than two years after the report was published, the Indonesian Government had begun to implement only one of these recommendations, with the establishment of a National Human Rights Commission. The government's failure to act on the Special Rapporteur's recommendations raises questions about the sincerity of its stated commitment to uphold international human rights standards. More important, it has meant that the root causes of torture and ill-treatment identified by the Special Rapporteur have yet to be addressed.

In early 1994, the Indonesian Government invited the Special Rapporteur on extrajudicial, summary or arbitrary executions to visit East Timor later in the year. It remains to be seen whether the government will cooperate fully with the Special Rapporteur, and whether it will implement any recommendations he might make.

The government has answered inquiries by all of the UN human rights thematic mechanisms. Unfortunately, its responses have not always been satisfactory. In 1992, the Working Group on Enforced or Involuntary Disapperances submitted the names of 207 "disappeared" East Timorese to the government for clarification. By late 1993, the government had supplied responses on only 20 cases. The Working Group considered only five of those responses to be satisfactory, noting in its December 1993 report:

"In the remaining 15 cases the names of the persons contained in the Government's reply did not correspond to the names...contained in the lists of the Working Group."[32]

In some cases the government has simply issued a blanket denial of violations reported. Responding to a letter from the same Working Group, the government claimed that "the allegation of

113

disappearances in Aceh...is clearly a fabrication, as there is no such thing as a 'general pattern of disappearances' in Aceh."[33] Following a long-established practice, the government also questioned the integrity and impartiality of those who have submitted the reports to the UN, rather than address the substance of the allegations. In the communication cited above, the government stated it was:

> "...displeased that partisan observers have submitted reports to the United Nations on allegations of human rights violations in Indonesia which are one-sided, unsubstantiated and not supported by the facts. Moreover, the allegations are exaggerated and based only on second-hand sources whose reliability is questionable."[34]

The government has taken a more positive attitude towards the work of other UN officials and bodies. The UN Secretary-General's Personal Envoy, Amos Wako, visited East Timor in February 1992 and April 1993. UN representatives were permitted to attend at least one session of the trial of Xanana Gusmão and, in January 1994, the government accepted a visit to Jakarta and Dili by a delegation from the UN Secretary-General's office. These moves suggested that the Indonesian Government has taken expressions of UN concern about East Timor to heart, and they should therefore be welcomed.

However, visits by the personal envoys or staff of the Secretary-General do not serve as a satisfactory replacement for the visits by the UN's human rights monitoring mechanisms recommended by the Commission on Human Rights. Because their mandates do not generally encompass human rights fact-finding, and their findings are generally not made public, such envoys do not provide the Commission or the international community with a basis for assessing the human rights situation in the territory. The decision not to release the findings from such visits also means that information about the conditions under which they are conducted cannot be made public. A more general problem is that such visits do not provide concrete recommendations, based on specific expertise, through which the human rights situation might be improved.

Restrictions on human rights monitoring

While the government claims to respect international human rights standards, it obstructs independent investigations of abuse.

CHAPTER 8

Despite some improvements in the past two years, continued restrictions on access to East Timor and to Aceh and other parts of Indonesia have made it difficult, if not impossible, for international and domestic human rights organizations to monitor the human rights situation.

Since the 1991 Santa Cruz massacre the government has frequently stated its commitment to improving access to East Timor by human rights and humanitarian organizations. That commitment was reiterated following a meeting between Indonesian and Portuguese government representatives in New York in December 1993, in a meeting between President Suharto and members of the US Congress in January 1994, and in April 1994 before the fourth round of UN-sponsored talks between Indonesia and Portugal.

There has been some progress on this front; East Timor is more open to outsiders now than at any time since 1975. Official delegations from the USA, Australia, Sweden, and the UN have been granted permission to visit East Timor in the past two years. However, such visits are tightly controlled by military authorities, and East Timorese who speak to foreign delegates risk detention and interrogation. Visitors who speak critically about their impressions of East Timor are condemned by the government, while those who echo the official position are quoted at international meetings and in the press.

The government record with regard to the ICRC has been equally mixed. On the positive side, it has extended the organization's access to political detainees both in East Timor and Indonesia. However, the government continues to deny access — or to delay granting it — where matters of "national security" are deemed to be at stake. The ICRC was able to conduct confidential prison visits in East Timor only sporadically between March and December 1992. In June 1993 it suspended visits to political prisoners in the territory for the third time in six months because of unacceptable restrictions imposed by the military. In early January 1994, the government suspended ICRC and family visits to Xanana Gusmão, after it was discovered that he had written letters to the International Commission of Jurists and the Portuguese Government.

The preoccupation with access to East Timor by international organizations and delegations has obscured an even more basic problem: that domestic human rights organizations continue to face restrictions on their work. Notwithstanding the President's call for greater political openness, more than 20 people have been jailed since late 1993 in connection with their non-violent human rights related activities, and others continue to serve prison terms.

The National Human Rights Commission

The National Human Rights Commission was established by Presidential Decree in June 1993 and its full complement of members was decided in December 1993. It carries out investigations in response to complaints from victims, lawyers, and independent organizations. Since it was established the commission has conducted investigations into a wide range of human rights violations, including several land and labour disputes, and a number of cases of political imprisonment and extrajudicial execution. The energy with which the commission began its task was encouraging, and it surprised critics with the strength of some of its public statements. However, there is serious doubt that it can meet the standards of impartiality and independence set by the UN, or that it can be effective in bringing a halt to serious human rights violations.

The commission's mandate is limited. Its main functions are to advise the government agencies responsible for the implementation of human rights policy, to engage in human rights education and to monitor the human rights situation in the country. While it may look into specific cases of human rights violations and carry out on-site inquiries, the commission has no formal powers of investigation and the government has no obligation to accept its recommendations or advice.

To date, the commission appears to have interpreted its mandate rather narrowly. In one of its first official acts, five members of the commission visited 11 of the 21 students arrested during a peaceful demonstration on 14 December 1993. In comments to the press, members of the commission noted that the students had been well treated by police, but they conspicuously failed to comment on the fact of their arrest and detention. Apparently, the commission did not consider imprisonment for the peaceful expression of political opinions to fall within its mandate. Members of the commission have sometimes made statements that appear to condone serious human rights violations. Commenting on "Operation Cleansing" in March 1994, commission member Bambang Suharto said:

> "*As long as it is done in line with existing procedures...the shooting of criminals can be understood...Which one is to*

be chosen, protecting the human rights of criminals or the victims of crime?"

The composition of the 25-member commission has given rise to concern about its independence. Chairman Ali Said, appointed by the President, is a retired military officer who has served as a military court judge, Minister of Justice, and Chief Justice of the Supreme Court. After the 1965 coup, he was the Chief Justice on the special military court which convicted the former Foreign Minister, Dr Subandrio, of subversion and sentenced him to death.[35] Proceedings in these special military courts failed utterly to meet international standards of fairness.

The Secretary-General of the commission is the current Director General of Corrections in the Ministry of Justice; this represents an apparent conflict of interest. The problems this could cause surfaced just weeks after the commission was formed, when the government announced that it had suspended visits to Xanana Gusmão by the ICRC and relatives. Despite the fact that the ban infringed UN principles for the protection of detainees, the Director General defended the decision, saying "I have to discipline him for disgracing the people and the nation of Indonesia."[36]

On the positive side, the commission's members include respected lawyers and legal scholars with no direct connection to the government or the military. It is nevertheless striking that the commission includes only one member of a non-governmental organization, and none of the country's best known human rights activists. According to available reports, prominent human rights activists declined to serve on the commission because they were not confident it would be able to function freely and independently.

Additional concern about the commission's independence arises from its legal status. Because it was established by presidential decree, Indonesian human rights experts have expressed concern that its survival remains subject to presidential approval. A related concern is that the commission is entirely funded by the state, raising questions about its independence.

The Government and Amnesty International

Amnesty International was officially barred from visiting Indonesia for more than 15 years following the 1977 publication of a report on political imprisonment in the country.[37] Relations have improved somewhat in recent years, but the government has continued to portray Amnesty International as a subversive organization, bent on undermining the New Order. While government officials have acknowledged in talks with Amnesty International that such allegations are without foundation, they continue unabated in official public statements and internal briefings.

Amnesty International's campaigns against human rights violations in Indonesia and East Timor are characterized as interference in the country's internal affairs. In June 1993, for example, a high-ranking Foreign Ministry official told journalists that an appeal for asylum by seven East Timorese at two embassies in Jakarta had been "engineered" by Amnesty International, citing a two-page appeal the organization had issued several hours after the asylum-seekers entered the embassies.

Despite the government's stated commitment to improving access to Indonesia and East Timor by international human rights organizations, Amnesty International continues to face serious obstacles. In January 1993 the government permitted an Amnesty International delegate to attend a UN human rights workshop in Jakarta. However, the delegate was allowed to stay for only five days, making any serious human rights investigation impossible. Requests for a visa extension were denied, as were requests to hold substantive talks with government officials. The government also refused Amnesty International's delegate permission to travel to East Timor to observe Xanana Gusmão's trial.

The government exploited Amnesty International's visit for political purposes. When improved access by international human rights organizations was demanded at the 1993 UN Commission on Human Rights the government falsely claimed that Amnesty International had already been allowed to visit without restriction and that the organization's delegate had held a press conference in Jakarta at which he made unacceptably critical remarks about Indonesia, and about the UN Workshop.

An Amnesty International representative was able to visit Indonesia in July 1993 and again in March 1994 to conduct research into human rights developments in selected areas of the country. The government was informed of these visits in writing. With respect to the July 1993 visit, a formal request was extended to meet government representatives in order to discuss issues of mutual concern, but the government did not respond. Shortly before the March 1994 visit, the government assured Amnesty International that it would soon be invited to visit Indonesia and East Timor, and

CHAPTER 8

in late April the Foreign Minister said the government hoped to open a dialogue with the organization. Amnesty International wrote to the government in May welcoming these statements and proposing a visit within the next two months. Regrettably, by mid-1994, the government had not replied.

9

Conclusions and recommendations

The structures, policies and attitudes which lie at the root of human rights violations in Indonesia and East Timor, and which have contributed to their institutionalization, have endured for almost three decades. The government, and particularly the military command at its political core, has persistently made it clear that basic human rights will be set aside in the name of national security, stability, order and development. Unchecked by domestic legal or political mechanisms, the security forces have continued to commit violations with impunity.

If human rights violations are to be prevented in the future, concrete steps must be taken to address their root causes. The chief responsibility for action rests with the Government of Indonesia. However, to the extent that they have acquiesced in the pattern of grave violations for more than a quarter of a century, members of the international community must also share responsibility.

Amnesty International offers the following set of 32 recommendations to the Government of Indonesia and to UN member states. If implemented, these measures could help improve the human rights situation in Indonesia and East Timor. The recommendations are grouped into three categories: those which would help to resolve or redress past and continuing violations; those which would help to prevent future violations; and those which would demonstrate the government's genuine commitment to the promotion of international human rights standards and their effective implementation.[38]

CHAPTER 9
Recommendations to the Government of Indonesia

I. Resolve and redress human rights violations

To resolve and redress past or continuing human rights violations in Indonesia and East Timor, Amnesty International urges the government to:

1. Establish the identity, the circumstances of death, and the whereabouts of the victims of all reported extrajudicial executions;

2. Permit independent human rights monitors, including forensic experts, to conduct thorough and impartial investigations of reported burial sites of the victims of all reported extrajudicial executions;

3. Promptly clarify the fate, or establish the whereabouts, of all those reported to have "disappeared" in custody;

4. Release immediately and unconditionally all prisoners of conscience — those held solely for the non-violent expression of their political or religious views;

5. Ensure that all those detained without charge in connection with their alleged political activities, are charged with a recognizably criminal offence and brought to trial promptly and fairly, or released;

6. Ensure the release, or the speedy and impartial review of the trials, of all those sentenced in unfair political trials;

7. Provide fair compensation to the victims of all human rights violations or, in the case of those killed or "disappeared", to their immediate relatives;

8. Ensure that the suspected perpetrators of human rights violations are brought promptly to justice before a civilian court, and that they are disarmed and suspended from active duty pending the outcome of the proceedings;

9. Abolish the death penalty, and commute all outstanding death sentences.

II. Prevent human rights violations

To prevent the occurrence of future human rights violations in Indonesia and East Timor, Amnesty International urges the government to:

1. Prohibit explicitly by law all extra-legal, arbitrary and summary executions and "disappearances" and ensure that any such executions are recognized as criminal offences and are punishable by penalties which take into account their seriousness;

2. Establish clear guidelines regarding the use of lethal force by government and government-backed troops in accordance with the UN Code of Conduct for Law Enforcement Officials;

3. Prohibit explicitly by law all forms of torture and other cruel, inhuman or degrading treatment or punishment, and ensure that all such acts are recognized as criminal offences, punishable by penalties which reflect the seriousness of the crime;

4. Guarantee that all detainees, including those held for suspected national security offences, are permitted prompt and regular access to lawyers of their choice, and to doctors and relatives;

5. Ensure that any person deprived of their liberty shall be held in an officially recognized place of detention and be brought before a judicial authority promptly after arrest;

6. Take all necessary steps, including the enforcement of existing legislation and the introduction of further legislation, to ensure that statements extracted under torture or other ill-treatment cannot be admitted as evidence during any legal proceedings, except against a person accused of torture as evidence that the statement was made;

7. Promptly repeal the Anti-Subversion Law and conduct a thorough review of all legislation pertaining to national security and public order to ensure that national security interests cannot be invoked to imprison people for the peaceful exercise of their right to freedom of expression;

8. Establish and maintain centralized public registers of all

detainees in all parts of the country, to be updated on a frequent and regular basis and made available to detainees' relatives, lawyers and the National Human Rights Commission;

9. Ensure that the mandate, terms of reference, composition and methods of work of the National Human Rights Commission conform to the standards enumerated by the UN Commission on Human Rights;

10. Ensure that suspected perpetrators are immediately disarmed and removed from active service pending the outcome of human rights investigations, and that they are promptly brought to justice before a civilian court.

III. Promote human rights

To demonstrate its commitment to promoting international human rights standards, and encouraging their full and effective implementation, Amnesty International urges the government to:

1. Invite the UN Working Group on Arbitrary Detention, and the UN Working Group on Enforced or Involuntary Disappearances to visit Indonesia and East Timor in the near future, in order to conduct a full investigation of the human rights situation;

2. Invite the UN Special Rapporteur on torture to conduct a follow-up visit to Indonesia and East Timor to assess implementation of the recommendations set out in his January 1992 report;

3. Accede to the ICCPR, its First Optional Protocol which permits the Human Rights Committee to receive individual complaints, and its Second Optional Protocol which requires State parties to take all necessary steps to abolish the death penalty;

4. Accede to the CAT and recognize the competence of the UN Committee against Torture to receive individual complaints and to hear inter-state complaints;

5. Permit the regular and unhindered monitoring of human rights in Indonesia and East Timor by domestic and

international human rights organizations, including Amnesty International.

Recommendations to UN Member States

In view of the grave concern about human rights in Indonesia and East Timor which has been expressed in a variety of UN fora, Amnesty International calls upon UN member states to:

1. Urge the Government of Indonesia to invite the UN Working Group on Arbitrary Detention, and the UN Working Group on Enforced or Involuntary Disappearances to visit Indonesia and East Timor;

2. Seek a systematic follow-up to the January 1992 report of the UN Special Rapporteur on torture on his visit to Indonesia and East Timor;

3. Seek a systematic follow-up to the report of the UN Special Rapporteur on extrajudicial, summary or arbitrary executions on his planned 1994 visit to Indonesia and East Timor;

4. Seek additional means to assure the regular and effective monitoring, under UN auspices, of the human rights situation in Indonesia and East Timor;

5. Urge the Indonesian Government to permit the regular and unhindered monitoring of human rights in Indonesia and East Timor by domestic and international human rights organizations, including Amnesty International;

6. Encourage the Government of Indonesia to accede to both the International Covenant on Economic, Social and Cultural Rights and the ICCPR, and its Optional Protocols;

7. Encourage the Government of Indonesia to accede to the CAT and recognize the competence of the UN Committee against Torture to receive individual complaints and to hear inter-state complaints;

8. Ensure that asylum-seekers are not forcibly returned to Indonesia if they would be at risk of serious human rights violations there, and ensure that the claims of all asylum-seekers, including those in detention, are fully and impartially assessed.

ENDNOTES

[1] The CGI was formed in 1992 after Indonesia disbanded its predecessor, the Inter-Governmental Group on Indonesia (IGGI), in response to human rights criticism by the Netherlands.

[2] The two parties are the *Partai Demokrasi Indonesia* (PDI) and the *Partai Persatuan Pembangunan* (PPP).

[3] *Jakarta Post*, 8 February 1994

[4] *Editor*, 4 July 1992

[5] *Jakarta Post*, 18 December 1993.

[6] *Kedaulatan Rakyat*, 29 August 1991

[7] *Kompas*, 5 August 1993

[8] *Jakarta Post*, 17 May 1991

[9] *Republika*, 3 January 1994

[10] *Jakarta Post*, 13 July 1993

[11] *Kompas*, 11 July 1991

[12] *Tempo*, 17 November 1990

[13] The organization's full name is *Aceh/Sumatra National Liberation Front*.

[14] *Republika*, 5 February 1993

[15] *Tempo*, 20 October 1990

[16] *Jakarta Post*, 8 May 1990

[17] *Reuters*, 25 November 1990

[18] *Ibid*

[19] *Editor*, 20 October 1993

[20] *Jakarta Post*, 23 November 1993

[21] *Suharto: Pikiran, Ucapan dan Tindakan Saya*, (Jakarta: PT Citra Lantoro Gung Persada, 1989), p. 364

[22] *Jakarta Post*, 25 April 1993

[23] *Tempo*, 3 July 1993

[24] *International Herald Tribune*, 3 May 1994

[25] The so-called "Torture Manual" was prepared under the auspices of the Military Resort Command KOREM/Wira Dharma in East Timor in 1982.

[26] Report of the UN Special Rapporteur on torture (E/CN.4/1993/26, p.62, para. 273)

[27] *Suara Merdeka*, 16 May 1993

[28] *Reuters*, 22 June 1991

POWER AND IMPUNITY

[29] Right of Reply by the Indonesian Observer Delegation on Item 12, UN Commission on Human Rights, 21 February 1990

[30] Letter from the President of Indonesia to the Secretary General of the Inter-Parliamentary Union, dated 4 September 1993

[31] Paragraphs 6 and 7 of a resolution adopted without a vote by the Inter-Parliamentary Council at its 153rd session (Canberra, 18 September 1993)

[32] Report of the Working Group on Enforced or Involuntary Disappearances, 22 December 1993 (E/CN.4/1994/26, p.66, para. 267)

[33] *Ibid*, para. 270

[34] *Ibid*, para. 268

[35] His sentence was formally commuted to life imprisonment in December 1980.

[36] *Jakarta Post*, 13 January 1994

[37] *Indonesia: An Amnesty International Report* (AI Index: PUB 77/00/77)

[38] Most of these recommendations are based on international human rights instruments, particularly the ICCPR and the CAT. Some are also based on standards set out in the UN Code of Conduct for Law Enforcement Officials; the Body of Principles for the Protection of All Persons under Any Form of Detention or Imprisonment; the Principles on the Effective Prevention and Investigation of Extra-Legal, Arbitrary and Summary Executions; and the Declaration on the Protection of All Persons from Enforced Disappearance.